A DANGEROUS WOMAN

Mother Jones, An Unsung American Heroine

BY MARCY HEIDISH

A Woman Called Moses

The Secret Annie Oakley

Witnesses

Miracles

The Torching

Deadline

ALSO BY MARCY HEIDISH

Who Cares? Simple Ways YOU Can Reach Out

A Candle At Midnight

Soul and the City

*Defiant Daughters: Christian Women of
Conscience*

A DANGEROUS WOMAN

Mother Jones, An Unsung American Heroine

A Novel

by Marcy Heidish

Dolan & Associates, Publishers

A Dangerous Woman
Mother Jones, An Unsung American Heroine

LIBRARY OF CONGRESS CATALOGING-IN-PUBLICATION DATA
Heidish, Marcy.
   A Dangerous Woman: Mother Jones, An Unsung American
Heroine.
     p.cm.
     ISBN:978-0-9792404-8-5
Library of Congress Control Number: 2010939277

Cover Photo: LOC Prints and Photographs Division; Reproduction
#LC-USZ62-7678; Mother Jones, Nov. 4, 1902; copyright by Bertha
Howell

Dolan & Associates, Publisher
Printed in the United States of America
....
First edition

As we come marching, marching in the beauty of the day,
A million darkened kitchens, a thousand mill lofts gray,
Are touched with all the radiance that a sudden sun discloses,
For the people hear us singing,'Bread and roses, bread and
    roses....'

As we come marching, marching, unnumbered women dead,
Go crying through our singing their ancient call for bread.
Small art and love and beauty their drudging spirits knew.
Yes, it is bread we fight for, but we fight for roses, too!
    — James Oppenheim – 1912

Pray for the dead — and fight like hell for the living!
    — "Mother" Mary Harris Jones

I figured I had a right to go free or die. I would have one or
    the other.
    — Harriet Ross Tubman

In Memoriam:

Harriet Ross Tubman

Anne Marbury Hutchinson

Annie Oakley Butler

Elizabeth Bailey Seton

PROLOGUE

« 1 »

Colorado, 1914.

Dawn.
The night train out of Denver slows between stations.
There is a brief "unauthorized" stop. No one notices me,
a small woman in black, as I step off the car. In moments,
I have disappeared down the dim road pluming ahead of
me, gray as a funnel of smoke.

Darkness drains from the air like dye from rinsed
cloth. The sky turns the color of my husband's eyes. I
shake that thought from my head and pull on my worn,
strong boots. They creak companionably as I tramp the
mile or so into Trinidad, Colorado. The strikers' camp lies
just beyond the town. I walk faster. Few pass; no one
glances up. The bank and the post office come into sight.
As I near the barber shop, the red-and-white pole starts
to spin. I begin to feel lucky — always a bad sign. And
sure enough, within minutes, there in the raw new light,
a man blocks my path.

I am stopped. Detained. Arrested.

Again.

This is not what I'd call a surprise. After all, I am defying the governor's order to stay out of "his" state. I just hadn't thought to be nabbed here so fast. First, I'd meant to visit the striking miners and their families — stir their spirits and give them support. Clearly, the governor and his boys don't want that to happen. I've misjudged them on one vital area: brains. After all these years, I seldom guess wrong, but there's no other way to see it.

Still, some arrests annoy the hell out of me.

This one, especially, and not only because I lost a round. There's something more serious afoot, now: I am to be jailed indefinitely — on no charges at all; without a warrant, without any suspicion of crime. No reasons, no rights, few words.

Ever heard of the Constitution, sonny? I burn to say that. Even so, I govern my tongue. I do not resist. I never resist. But I can damn well glare. Unfazed, the fresh-faced young soldier is downright solicitous as he clicks the cuffs on me.

"Can I take your arm, Ma'am?"

"No," I snap back. "You can take my suitcase."

"Far from home?" He tries again.

"Home's here now."

"Here?" He stares.

"Let's go." I'm in no mood to explain.

My address is like my shoes, it travels with me. And I'm always on the move. Wherever there's a good fight for rights, I just have to have to jump in. Sometimes that takes me to Washington, DC, or the Carolina mills, up to Minnesota or out to Wyoming, or here in the Colorado coal fields. I've had no fixed residence for a long while, nor do I want one anymore. That's done, that's gone. An odd way of life for a woman, perhaps, but it suits me well.

In Ireland, where I was born, I might be called a bit of a rover; a rambler; a chancer. But rovers drift; I drive. Or else I'm driven, my critics say. Let them talk. I come from hardworking people and I've always worked hard myself. Before I took up with labor causes, I was a licensed teacher and a trained seamstress. I refuse to respond to false rumors about other professions — like the one that says I ran a Denver brothel years ago.

That one's a corker.

I'd never solicit for prostitutes.

I'd be more likely to organize them.

~~

Now my address is this jail cell in Walsenburg, Colorado, where I am still held without charges; without bail. Status quo for someone like me: A Labor leader. A humanitarian? No: A hell-raiser.

For the present my work is simple: waiting it out.

Almost one month has passed since I began this writing. I started it as a report of the coal strike out here. But I get no news, so I can't keep an account. Martial law rules in this area and God only knows when it will end. As long as the strikers hold out, Governor Elias Ammons wants to shut me up; he's made no secret of that.

There's not a subtle bone in that man's body.

There's not much stretch to his thinking, either.

And I would hardly number him among my friends.

"You're the most dangerous woman in America," Ammons told me.

"That's stale talk," I reminded him.

"You crook you finger and a thousand contented men lay down their jobs."

"Contented!" I sputtered.

"A dangerous woman," he repeated.

It's a circular conversation, to put it politely, and we've had it several times. The governor is fond of quoting the West Virginia District Attorney who invented that title for me. It must have a certain ring to it — the press goes to it like flies to pie: those words stream above my photos in the papers. The contrast between pictures and print is almost too rich.

And isn't it a hell of a good laugh?

"The Most Dangerous Woman in America" does not look the part. In the mirrors, I see a sweet-faced old lady, the kind who knits mittens for missionary societies. I stand five feet tall. My spectacles are steel and my hair is silver. My dress is always black, long, and old-fashioned. I favor a bit of lace at the throat — and pansies, for luck, on my black hat. And I never go hatless. I make my own clothes; always have. No Godey's Ladies Book patterns for me. I've sewn for the wealthy and for the poor, and I've taught school in more than one state.

I believe there's still a bit of that school-marm about me. I see it in the prim, firm way I hold myself for the camera. Teaching has been a grand preparation for what I do now. I am used to standing up and speaking out, chiding and challenging; changing some minds. My brogue is nearly gone and when I make speeches, I have a "singing voice," according to Mr. Carl Sandburg. My favorite poet. Who else? Only the great Robert Burns. But Mr. Sandburg has never heard me speak when I am riled. He sees me as most do, at first glance: a grand-motherly figure, as much as a school-marm.

Of course, this figure is not entirely without design.

My appearance is my ticket to travel. I appear so damn harmless, I usually get in wherever I wish, no questions asked. I can stare down a gun barrel and dare some goon to shoot me. No one wants to blow the head off a "lady" who resembles his very own mother. I pass where few women of authority go: mines, mills, meetings where I take the podium. There, beyond the poet's hearing, I've been known to talk rough with rough men — if that's the language I need to reach them. It often serves me well to swear like a sailor and act like an auntie.

I'd bet that I'm the only woman in the world who *adds* years to her age for effect. It's part of my power to look venerable. I was in my forties when I began organizing laboring folk but early on my hair went white — shock it was, from the bad times that twice wrenched my life. I seldom speak of them; they cut too deep. In any case, I think they aged me — not in strength, but in looks. No rouges or dyes for me, though. I do nothing to detract from my maternal appearance. And for years, the people and the press have referred to me as "Mother." It's become a part of my name: "Mother Jones."

Only a few close friends call me by my baptismal name: Mary, eldest daughter of Richard Harris, rebel and railroad man, and Ellen Cotter, a housekeeper. I was also Mary Jones, wife of George Jones, a master iron molder and father of four. Mary, I am to twenty-three cousins and sister to four. That includes the well-known priest, William Harris, who has cast me off for my "unseemly" behavior — not to mention my criticisms of clergy and the church. Isn't it odd how Billy is called "Father" and I am called "Mother" but there's not one living child belonging to us, not anymore.

Never mind. She's gone, that young Mary Harris Jones — she of the tossing red hair and the snapping blue eyes. Pretty, she was called. 'Darlin,' she was called. Mother, she was called that, too, but the word meant something different back then.

There I must stop myself and change tack. There's too much pain in remembering. I savor the present and seal the past.

~~

For thirty some years, I've lived in the moment and I've traveled light, as far as possessions go, that is.

At the time of this recent arrest, I had little to confiscate:

One spare black dress.
One black wool shawl.
One pair black shoes.
One thimble, two needles.
One spool black thread.
One pocket watch, still ticking.
One purse; two handkerchiefs.
Two hat pins, six hairpins.
Assorted "unmentionables."

It made me damn mad when they took away my spectacles. Soon enough, though, I had everything back — save for the needles and the hat-pins. I suppose they were classed as "weaponry." I can just imagine the headlines: *Mother Jones, Armed and Dangerous.*" Thank God I'm not permitted to see the newspapers here, or I'd be in a constant whirl of fury. I don't even try to get the papers smuggled in, as I did with this pad, pen and ink. I've never been too proud to bribe a guard when the need arises.

Mostly, it does.

Sure, I've been locked up before — but this is the worst place I've ever been. It's no accident that I've been stashed into this basement cell; cold, dank, stinking of mold. The governor thinks to sicken me here, I believe, and he just might manage it: I'm seventy-seven, that's the truth, and he's thinking I'm done; pneumonia hit me hard last year. Until then, I was strong as a workhorse, no matter the weather, no matter my age.

In these grand boots, I've tramped the hills of West Virginia at Christmastime. I'd hate to think I'll never be doing that again. When I arrived in Colorado, the weather was flukey and fair. Now it's March and a harsh one, too. This cell is a sieve to the winds and there's more snow yet to come.

Not that I'm complaining. I disapprove of whining, even on paper. I've spent countless nights in workers' unheated shacks, sleeping on the floor with my purse for a pillow. One February, I wangled a job in a textile mill, so I could see the working conditions firsthand. Right off, I was shown to the company's housing — the kind most mills have. It was a scarcely a shack, with great holes in the windows and walls. The company man shrugged these off: How cool this "house" will be in the summer, he said, straight-faced. He didn't even blink. Such memories boil my blood, even now.

In any case:

It's not the cold I fear here, nor the discomfort; nor even the rats. Hell, I've seen their like before, strutting the streets in fine suits of clothes, and I'm only half-joking. These sewer rats — they're big, but not so hard to best. In a corner of this cell, I found a broken beer bottle and hid it in my skirts. Then I learned how to use the bottle as a club; I wielded it in a clear case of self-defense. I don't want those creatures skittering over my face in the night or nibbling at my fingers. I'll put up with a lot but there's got to be a line drawn somewhere. In my case, it's rats.

This is the drill, then:

I wait.

I aim.

I clobber.

The trick is this: I hold still, scarcely breathing. I let the varmints draw near. And when they start to sniff at my hem, I smack them squarely on the head. I'm thinking my technique shows some improvement. I've knocked out six rats and struck two of them silly; I keep a daily count of such small victories. I count these — and I count days.

If I had been charged I'd know what I'm up against. Limbo is never a likable state. My friends are talking with union lawyers. Still, the governor could make my stay a long stretch. He's not the only one who wants me silenced — there are others, I know, who are wanting the same. Rockefeller, for one; his family owns the coal companies here. West Virginia's governor, for another. I could go on. How convenient for them if I weakened and died here, ever so quietly.

In case that happens, I keep at my writing. This is not another "open letter," leaked to the press, about this long strike. I had that one smuggled out, weeks ago.

Now I write for myself.

I need to remind myself who I am and who I have been. And I guess I need to get back on speaking terms with the past. One day — God willing — I'll pen a different kind of autobiography: the "public" kind. What I write now is different. For my own peace, I want to take an inner inventory: what I have done, and how, and why.

Did it all matter, really? Has my work made any real difference? I'm no longer so sure, as once I was. For the first time, damn it, I truly feel old. And if I think back, honestly, I have lost as many fights as I have won. This incident in Trinidad just drives that truth home. Perhaps my life has only been that of a rover's, after all. I hate that thought; still, I must find out. I can't go on any longer, carrying doubts. As I've said, I prefer to travel light.

~~

Each night now, I sit up late in the buttery light of one small oil lamp. My black shawl covers my shoulders. One hand holds a pen, the other, that bottle. Beyond the circle of lamplight, there is a wall of darkness. Behind it, I can hear rustlings and twitters. The damp grasps me like a fist. My pen pauses, then scratches on.

It's rare that I have time to reflect on my life. It's rare that I want to do so as all. Such scrutiny is like plumbing the depths of a well and that, we all know, carries the risk of tumbling in. I easily could take such a fall in this place.

Again, the old dreams slice into my sleep. I wake, shaking, and fumble for the lamp. I light in on the third or fourth try, then gaze about the cell. My black dress is draped over a stool, and my black hat hangs motionless, and my black shoes are still. I scan the darkness for Mother Jones and cannot always find her now. She is my savior, in a way, as much as she has been that for others — at her best. I need her strength now. Instead, I find my own weakness.

Here is the real peril to me — here is what I fear most: Those long blank nights and endless, empty days.

They are pure poison to one like myself: always moving, always doing; seldom alone. I fear this enforced idleness more than the pneumonia; more than the chance that I could be hanged on some trumped-up charge. Above all, I fear that I have been thrown back across my well-crafted borders, to the Mary Harris Jones I fled for so long. That unseen Mary who had — what?

Nothing.

No one.

Nowhere to go.

But survival seems to be my stock in trade, after all. Is that blessing or curse? I have pondered this question to no avail. It is, as my mother would say, "an abiding wonderment." Whatever it is, I have got it in good supply. Survival against the odds: That appears to be my kinfolk's gift. And how I have raged and wept when this gift has not spread beyond us to others. Still, raging and weeping have never gotten me very far. Nor do they change this stubborn thing in the blood, in the bone; in the soul.

I know this because of the rope factory.

It comes back to me here, after so many years. Once I got myself hired on in such a place — again, to survey working conditions. I recall the people, the mill, the town. But what I remember most clearly is this: The raw power of the stuff supporting them all — simple twine. It's so thin in the hand; and so fibrous, so tough, so capable bearing great weight. I sense something similar running through my own people to me. I must see if this is true — or just fanciful comfort. One way or the other, I have to know.

Here is what I will do, then:

I will test that twine.

If it is mine, it will bear me up.

And on its strength, I will swing myself out and out and out — over the deep and dangerous well of the past.

■

PART ONE

« 2 »

C ork City, 1843.

Night.
A knock at the door jolts me awake.
It's that strange knock: two raps, then three.
I sit straight up in the bed I share with my sister.
The knock comes again, exactly the same way.
I hear whispers, then my father's footsteps. They are heavy, however he tries to walk light. A strapping tall man is Rich Harris, with a head of thick black hair. Now his steps move to the clothespress; from there, to the threshold of our house. Swiftly and softly, the door clicks shut. Outside in the street, the neighborhood boy on lookout whistles. A cart approaches, slows, and rumbles away.
Inside, by the hearthstone, there is the clack-clack of my mother's pacing, and the faint tick of her Rosary beads. I am only six years old but I am alert to this sudden series of sounds. It is a pattern I've come to expect, at least one a fortnight. Now, somewhere in the

darkness of Cork, my father rides with nameless men, bound together by secret oaths.

In a bone-chilling voice, Mam has warned us, *Never a word of your Da going out, d'ye hear.* My small, fair, gentle mother looked so fierce, we heard her indeed — and "shut our gobs," as Mam might say.

Most of what I know has been gleaned by careful eavesdropping, late at night. And in the clothespress, by daylight, I have spied the small gemlike badge of green silk on a pin. This, I've discovered, is worn by my father when he steals out late. Only once have I seen it in his big rough hand, when I peered around the curtain dividing our rooms. The lookout had signaled from the street: *all clear.* As my father went out, Mam was making the sign of the Cross by the hearth. I imagine she does this whenever my father vanishes into the night. Still, I've not dared to spy on my parents again.

Now I lie back in our bed but my eyes will not close.

"Where's Da gone?" my sister whimpers.

"Hsshht" I warn her. "We can't be asking."

"You know. You saw him." Her voice starts to rise.

"He's out with his friends, nothing more."

"Why can't he tell us, then?"

"Secret, it is, now hsshht, Marta, hsshht."

We listen to my mother, steadily pacing. Like a clock's tick, the sound seems to lull my sister back to sleep. I stay awake, a bit frightened; a bit thrilled. In my head, I go over all that I've heard, all that I've noticed, all that I've pieced together about these strange nights: I never know when they will come but they do not vary.

Well after dark, the cart nears our house and my father jumps on. The cart gains speed then, I know, rolling out beyond the city limits, into the countryside of West Cork. There, in an empty barn, or what my father refers to as a "Safe House!" there is a meeting of a "brotherhood:" a secret society, outside the law. There have been many in this county, often called "Rebel Cork:" the Whiteboys, the Steelboys, the Defenders — and the Ribbonmen, known by their green silk badges.

Catholic patriots all, they stand against our British rulers and the wealthy lords who took over most of our land, long ago. We farm the land, my father says. We grow the crops, but we pay in potatoes for what's ours, by rights. I listen intently to this kind of talk. Sometimes, I know, the patriots take revenge on certain landlords: those who bleed tenant farmers with punishing rents. A storehouse may burst into flame; cattle may be turned loose. Mayhem, my mother calls this, and shudders. It's far more than that, my father tells her. Like the Whiteboys before them, the Ribbonmen fight other wrongs.

In fact, they helped stir up Cork's Tithe Wars, only two years before I was born. In a low, thrilling voice, my father likes to tell of the "Rathcormac Massacre." He becomes so excited, I just know he was there. In my mind, I can see it: There is my father, a great hill of a man, younger, even stronger, with that "Harris fire" in his light eyes. He had a fiery temper on him, as well, though he could be gentle and poetic at times. Growing up in North Cork, he had learned to be scrappy, but a line from a song could move him to tears. A natural rebel was my father. Of course, he was there at Rathcormac, protesting tithes on Catholics, even under gunfire.

I wish I still had my father's ribbon. I wish had gone out with him, or the grandfather I never knew. A member of the Whiteboys, he was hanged for supposed "rebellious activities." Like many a Catholic strung up on a tree, my grandfather was murdered without any official reaction or record. His men cut him down. His women waked him. And his story, in whispers, was passed along.

I think of green silk as I wait in this jail.

~~

Now, in my cell, the rats scuttle near as I eat my supper: black bread, pale broth, weak tea. No complaints. I remember when this would have been a banquet, indeed.

Those years press forward. For me, words still come hard when I think of that time. This is the way the oldest ones tell it; this is the way they say it began:

Up from the wild seas there rose a great mist and it shrouded the whole of the green, growing land. And when that mist lifted and vanished at last, it left the potato stalks blighted and limp. A terrible blackness covered the fields and black was the stench that clung to them all. Now, like a spell, a hush folded down over each village, as everyone watched the crops rotting away. No rains could cleanse the stalks of their darkness and no winds could breathe life into them again.

Was this God's scourge — or the wrath of the Devil? Nobody knew and none had the strength to reckon it out. None could make sense of what happened that year. Calves were born stunted. Chickens turned scrawny. Apples were small. Rents, paid in kind, were thricefold delayed. In those days, when children grew too wan to play, when parents grew to weak to laugh, even the hearthfires seemed to burn dim.

So it was across Ireland, that sinister summer of 1845, and so it was for five years thereafter, save one. People ate their seed potatoes, and what eggs were laid, and what scraps were found, and what game was poached, and what apples fell. The fields went black again — and yet again.

There was a cruel winter, burying turf piles in rare snow. Tenant farmers, behind in their rent, were forced from their cottages. Families, wandering, begged in the lanes. Some built shelters of branches and reeds: these we called "famine huts," and into them people crowded together to die. Thousands of starving folk made for the towns. Silent, spectral crowds clogged the roads. Along the way, some people sank to their knees and ate grass. There was a green tinge to their mouths when they died, while the curs and carrions circled close.

An Gort Mor, it was called.

The Great Hunger.

I knew it, I felt it; I grew up in those years.

When the first blight took hold, I was a child turning eight. When the famine ended, I was a young woman, just gone fourteen. I felt older than I was; all of us did, I suppose. With our own eyes we had seen the hordes of skeletal people, staggering up the road into Cork City. We had seen the green lips of the corpses piled in the streets and all night, we had heard the death carts grinding past. In disbelief, we had stared at the ships, loaded with mutton and butter and grain, sailing out of Cork Harbor. And we knew of — and loathed — Sir Charles Trevelyan, the British official charged with "Irish Relief."

Yes, there were scattered soup kitchens, dispensing greasy watered-down broth. Yes, there were some work gangs, for people too starved to work. These paltry efforts soon faded away. According to Trevelyan, the famine's chastisement could only "improve" Ireland's lax moral character.

Those words sparked my first real rage. Never before had I been so angered at forces beyond my own small circle. I was hot with this anger for a long while, until my father warned that this could consume me. Slowly, I cooled down, just enough to go on.

And after we emigrated, we seldom — if ever — spoke of that time. Those who lived through it rarely did so. Most of us could not bear to relive what had happened to our people. Few of us had words to speak the unspeakable: One million dead, two million gone, in half a dozen

years.   Since then, we measured time in two distinct
ways.
   There was "Before the Famine."
   And there was "After."
   I still think in these terms, even now.
   There's no way around it.
   I belong to both sides of that sharp divide.

                              ~~

Here is a "Before:"
   There came a surprise gift, the year I was seven — the
longest, sweetest summer in anyone's memory. It was too
rare, too lovely to cost us nothing, but we didn't think like
that then. None could imagine what would soon befall us.
All we saw was a summer like no other: a borrowed
season from a better world.
   Bewitched, that season was. It had the fullest moons,
the nearest stars, the softest days. Hedges bloomed twice
over with roses, cabbage-sized, the colors of butter and
brandy and brick. The late afternoon sun set the tall
grasses to flaming: entire fields on fire with such fierce
glory, it was not of this earth. Once, I pointed to a cloud,
just as the hidden sun haloed it. All summer, after that,
my sister begged me to point at the sky and "call out the
shine." But shine there was everywhere: in silvery
waters, in cobwebs glittering with dew, and on the fields,
pearly-green.
   Was there danger in the magic light? If there was, we
didn't notice. The cloud's huge shadows slid over us,
casting their shapes across the lands of Inchigeelagh,
where we passed our summers with my mother's people,
the Cotters. Toon's Bridge and Inchigeelagh perch along
the River Lee valley, thirty miles from Cork City, by the
carriage road. Pilgrims came there every summer, to dip
in the holy waters of Gougane Barra, where Saint
Finbarr, it was said, worked miraculous healings.

Ourselves, we dipped in the long strand of lakes, strung through purple hills and dark green furze that hid us at our games. In Irish, the village name means, "Isle of the Sheeps' Pen," and sheep there were, like small clouds themselves, seen from afar.

We were proud that the Cotter name was an old one in the parish of Inchigeelagh, along with Creedons, Luceys, and Kellehers. For centuries, Cotters had grown potatoes on small plots here, rented out in smaller and smaller parcels by the Protestant landlords. Despite them, we thought of this countryside as Cotter territory — our very own.

In truth, the O'Learys had been chieftains here — before the invasions of Cromwell and King William. The Cotters had endured through the Penal Laws that crushed Catholic rights, and through a failed uprising in 1798. And they hoped with the rise of Daniel O'Connell, "the Great Liberator."

I was struck by the power of his words, when I heard him speak. He could lift a crowd onto its feet. My family admired O'Connell; but they did not see him as a lasting savior. The Cotters had seen fortunes rise and fortunes fall. They simply went on with their sowing on St. Brigid's Day, the first of February, and their planting, on the Feast of St. Patrick, and their reaping at the Assumption of our Lady, mid-August. They stacked turf for winter and danced at the fairs, and they listened to the people talk by the fire.

From the time I can remember, there was my grandmother Cotter — she with the snapping blue eyes like my own. It was Gran who taught us hearthside history in the thatched, whitewashed cottage where she was born. If ever there was a "singing voice," it was hers. An outsider once called the Cotters' homes "hovels." My brother threw sod at them as they passed on. To us, these dwellings were neat whitewashed shelters, sacred and snug, scented with Gran's pipe smoke and her sweet turf fires.

"Ignorant," she called those travelers, I remember. It was Saturday night, which meant baths and blackberries with clotted cream — and for the grownups, dances at the crossroads. Fiddlers and pipers tossed tunes to the moon and the *bodhran*'s beat thrummed in my chest. My grandmother watched, smoking her clay pipe and, beneath her black skirts, her tall black boots kept time to the music.

Few country matriarchs had real boots or shoes like Gran. She was like a queen to our way of thinking and so this rarity did not surprise us. If she had truly "called out the shine" from the skies, we would not have been surprised at her powers.

It would always be like this, we believed.

We would always run barefoot through purple heather. We would always eat potatoes from the iron cauldron.

There would always be buttermilk and soda bread.

We would always eat together and sing after supper, old songs like *God of the Mighty Clans* and paeans to my grandmother's cooking:

> *Did you ever eat Colcannon*
> *Made with yellow cream*
> *And green leeks and potatoes*
> *Like a picture in a dream?*

We did.

Every summer we stepped into that picture. We were poor, true enough, but we did not seem to know it.

Until I was eight years old, I felt rich.

Summers, we had the Cotters' clan; winters, we belonged to another: the city folk of North Cork, where my father was born. I realize now that this was only a slum, but at the time, it was only "home." Our slice of a house looked like all the others, faced with red sandstone and crammed together on Cork's northside.

Not far off was the English Market, where my father worked for a time, unloading slick fish and sweet apples, pigs heads and peppercorns. I was born in the shadow of Shandon Church and I used to gaze up at its famous clock tower. The "Four-Faced Liar" we called it; each clock face told a different time. That's North Cork for ya, our neighbors said.

We children were wise to its twining lanes and it narrow alleys. We never got lost, or felt lost; never once. We knew its ways and its sounds.

"New milk — fresh eggs," voices called.

"Good ale, ripe fruit," others sang out.

"Violets, roses, for all your sweet lasses."

Each morning, I woke to the rumble of carts and the shouting of peddlers. Hogs snorted, rooting around in the street for scraps. Chickens squawked at the dogs who barked back. Beggars and rovers sang at the corners and after noon, red-faced men lurched from the pubs. If I turned right I could walk to the tannery — easy to find by its sharp odor. If I turned left, I could walk to the busy Cork Butter Market, where donkeys and carts were laden with barrels. Here, my broad-shouldered father worked a second job, hefting such shipments down to the docks along the River Lee.

All through the day, neighbors watched over us. From their windows, the women called out to us children as we played in the lanes. Washing swung on the lines strung across alleyways. Scallions and chives grew in pots on the sills and from the chimney tops, sparrows sang. Whenever we opened our door, familiar smells rose to greet us: leather and saddle-soap, coal-smoke and cabbage, whiskey and dung. Everyone knew everyone else — the streets were just an extension of home.

Throughout each day, the bells of St. Anne's told us the time. They chimed each quarter hour, no matter the weather, no matter the times — even after the first potato crop blackened and died.

That blight did not shake our city much, at least not right away. That year, we were caught up in our own household, where we welcomed a new baby's birth. The birthing was easy, the baptism merry — though the feast, I noticed, seemed a bit frugal.

My father went on working at the Market. The city around us still held food and jobs. No need to fret, everyone said: next year would be different.

This proved to be true.

It was far worse.

That winter was harder than anyone could recall. It brought heavy snow — rare in Cork, perched as it is in the south. That summer, the fields went black again and across Ireland a second potato crop failed totally. Then there came more frightening news: some of the Cotters, owing back rent, were forced from their homes. Gran flatly refused to quit her cottage — the constables burned the thatch roof over her head. Her fatal stroke came of the shock, we were told.

My uncle Tim brought us Gran's famous black boots.

There was a wake — with donated whiskey, to our shame.

There was a donated funeral ham — more shame, still.

There was a cardboard box for a coffin — shame, yet again.

And then a strange stillness flooded our house, filling it to the roof, as if with water. Even the baby seemed to cry less. We lived with a constant sense of foreboding. More upheavals, more losses, were yet on their way. I think we all felt them as they drew near to us, but no one dared put such thoughts into words. We said the Rosary every evening, as always. Our Holy lamp still glowed by the door. Each night, Mam raked the hearth and said a prayer for protection. Even so, we lay awake, waiting for the next shock.

This came more quickly than we could have guessed.

Neighbors, long known, began disappearing.

The McCarthys, next door, gave their eldest son an "American Wake" — a sendoff for someone sailing west, toward the new land. Eamon McCarthy would never return, we all knew that. We'd not be seeing him ever again. The very next day, he left on a ship out of Cobh Harbor. Cobh. No one could know how often that name would come to be spoken, or how many souls would depart from its docks.

The O'Sullivans sent their second son off.

The Collins boy, Jamey, was the next to depart.

The Doolin brothers sailed a week later, taking their fiddles with them to the ship, and we heard their voices shouting farewells.

It was always the menfolk who seemed to go first. We waited for each new departure with dread. Faces were missing, voices were gone. The street was changing. North Cork was changing. Our entire world went on changing — and fast. Too fast.

I remember the night when my father took out his savings from under the mattress. They shone in the lamplight that lay on the bed. Transfixed, we stared at the glittering coins. My mother turned her face from them and wept.

"Now, Nell." My father kept saying. "Don't take on."

"Isn't it right for me to be weeping?"

"Now Nell..." All other words seemed swept from his mind.

"Where are you off to, then?" She asked at last.

"Wherever there's work, so."

"How will we ever manage now, Rich?"

"Trust me, Nell, I'll send you money each week."

"But will you not be coming home?"

A silence snapped open like a torn seam.

"I'll send for you all," my father said finally. "It won't be long."

"We're all to leave Ireland?" Mam went pale.

"What choice is there, love?"

As if in answer, a warning whistle came from the neighborhood lookout, down the street. We heard boots tramp near. One glance outside was more than enough. The dreaded Royal Constabulary were nearing our house. What happened next came in a blur:

My father, swiftly bagging his few bright coins. My mother laying pressing his small green badge in his big hand. A flurry of footsteps cut off the stairway. My father jumped the low fire in the broad hearth; we heard him climbing brick by brick up the chimney.

When the constables banged on the door, the clothespress was closed, the hearth was clear, and my mother stood firm before it. We ran to her then, and clung to her skirt. The men burst into the room, overturning a chair. I cannot remember their faces — only the brass buttons on their uniforms. What I do recall is the sound of their voices; they spoke to us as we'd speak to dogs.

"Richard Harris?" The constable's eye swept the place.

"Not home, sir." Mam, just five feet tall, drew herself up.

"We'll see about that." The constable spat out the words.

"Please do," said my mother, keeping her voice even and clear.

The clothespress was emptied onto the floor. Doors were jerked open; curtains torn down. Bedding and clothing were tossed in the air. The place was a shambles when the men left — without finding a trace of one

Richard Harris, nor the ribbon that would have marked him as an outlaw.

We reckoned that he had emerged from the chimney and jumped roof to roof, until he got away. A messenger told us he'd made it to Cobh Harbor and sailed the next day. Now a new life began — without my father. Such a life seemed unreal and impossible, those first few days. Everywhere we looked, we found him missing and I realized how his strong presence had quietly ruled the house.

Soon we would join Da, my mother repeated. She saith this so often, I think that she was trying to convince herself.

Mam took in washing and scrubbed strangers' floors, while we children tried to help with the household. We burned the bread and over-cooked turnips, made lumpish beds and scrounged for coal. The baby survived our clumsy tending as did the small windowsill garden. The days were too busy for fretting, we found.

Still, in the nights, I would toss in my sleep, and wake up, shaking. I would steal from the bed to check the red glow of the holy lamp, burning before the picture of the Sacred Heart of Jesus. Now I was fearful that it might go out. Next, I would turn to the hearth, making sure that the banked embers still burned. No hearth was ever allowed to go cold. That happened only in empty houses — deserted homes. There were more and more of those, now, all around us.

Sometimes Mam would sit up with me. Never did she scold or order me back to bed. I would lean against her and she'd lean against me, and in the faint warmth, we'd rock together, as we sang — not hymns, not prayers, but that old song to Gran's favored dish:

> *Did you ever eat Colcannon*
> *Made with yellow cream*
> *And leek and fair potatoes*

Like a picture in a dream....

It was a long time before we ate anything like that again.

It's a mercy that we both lacked the gift of "The Sight." Our song would have choked us if we'd seen ahead.

~~

The day my mother boiled the boots, I knew we might die.

We had lived through four years of famine without my father, though he sent us money when he could. We could not imagine him in a place called Canada, where it was cold and where he worked on the railroad. Nor could he imagine what his native city had slowly become. Every day, we walked past bodies sprawled in the streets. The death carts cleared out other neighborhoods first.

I remember the stench; I remember glancing up at blank, boarded windows. Half our neighbors had sailed out of Cobh or died from the fevers that swept through North Cork. My mother still worked at her "scrub jobs," as we called them; she still took in laundry, as well. Our home resembled a kind of washhouse. With Mam, I wrung out the drawers and the shirts of the few rich folk who lived where we could walk with our laundry baskets.

Each evening, at prayers, Mam prayed that our health and our strength would continue. The fire in her, passed down from the Cotters, did not seem to go out. Worried, she watched us, scanning each face. My sisters and brother looked peaked and spindly; their voices had grown reedy and thin.

When I bothered to look in the glass, all I saw was a knife of a nose between jutting cheekbones. My eyes appeared glazed, like everyone else's. I felt strangely numb, listless, indifferent. Was I stunned or just starving? Both, I suppose.

In that state of shock, I believe, we chose to stay. Otherwise we'd go mad, like flame-haired Mrs. Larkin, who raved as she wandered the lanes with wild dogs. Her bitter laughter chilled the blood in my veins. Not long before, one of us would have taken her in. Now, where once we looked after each other, everyone looked away. We all hoarded food-scraps and tallow and lard. We climbed from moment to moment, just hanging on.

Each morning, I went to the market and bought what little I could for the family. Lentils, sometimes, would do for the day. Oatmeal could stretch over several meals. But the day that we feared arrived at last. Our employers paid late for their laundry, and there were few scrub-jobs now to be had. That week there was no money, by post, from my father. There was no food at all in the house.

That evening, my mother took Gran Cotter's boots out of the clothespress and studied them for a very long time. There were two pairs — for Sundays and weekdays. I stared from Mam to the boots and back again. My mother's flower-like mouth had closed tight as a day-lily at night. No words were spoken but I knew what would be happening next.

At five the next morning, Mam set the iron cauldron of water to boil on the hearth. We stared at the cauldron, recalling how it had cooked our potatoes, day after day, all of our lives.

At five-thirty, my mother dropped each of Gran's boots, one by one, into the steaming water, and added some boric acid to remove the shellac.

At five that evening, the cauldron was emptied, leather rinsed clean, drained dry, kneaded — and ready to cook.

Through those twelve hours, my mother said nothing, but her silence was a power, filling the house. As the day had gone on, she'd stirred the cauldron and done the mending. We'd heard the pot spit as she refilled it. The sound of the boiling seemed to grow louder; an odd dark smell hung near the hearth. Mam stirred the cauldron once more and kept her jaw set. We were a bit frightened of her, I think. This was some fierce stranger we did not know. Gentle Nell, she was called, soft as butter.

But not that day — she with her fair hair coming down, and a shine like the dew on her face, and a storm-like fury in her gray eyes. Frightened we were — of her and of what finally happened to us. The misery outside had come through the door and into our home, to crouch by our hearth. From our country summers, we remembered Gran's boots tapping to fiddlers who played jigs and reels. We watched in awe as Mam sharpened her knife. I remember the flash of late sun on the blade.

For a moment that knife seemed to hang in the air. Then it flashed again and struck the leather on the cutting board. My mother cut the boots into small pieces, seasoned them well with pepper and salt, doused them with broth, and mixed the pieces with sliced turnips. Summoning us with a mighty look, she lifted her ladle to dole out our portions.

"Stew." She threw out that word like a dare.

"Stew." We took the dare and held out our trenchers.

We sat to table. Mam said the same blessing as ever.

"For what we are about to receive...."

Upright in her hand, she held the ladle like a bishop's crook.

"May the Lord make us truly thankful...."

We could hear ourselves breathing.

"Through Jesus Christ, our sweet Savior."

She waited a moment.

"Amen," we chorused at last.

We took that meal without speaking. Spoons clinked against the wooden trenchers. Somebody coughed out in the street. A dog yelped, then howled. Our chewing seemed loud and unbearably thorough. That was the longest meal of my life. But I have to admit, when Mam excused us and our benches scraped back, we all felt full — and nobody had the nerve to get sick.

I helped my mother empty the cauldron outside the door. Then she wiped her hands on her apron and touched my hair. Soon, in the firelight, we prayed the Rosary, just before bedtime. As always, Mam sprinkled Holy Water on each of our faces as we lay in bed. I know what she wanted to tell us that night: No matter what, she would not let us starve. And one thing more. One thing above all:

"Never forget." Her voice scorched the dark.

"No, Mam," we promised.

I'm willing to swear that none of us did.

■

C olorado, 1914

"*Free Mother Jones!*"

In a cold breeze, banners ripple and voices rise.

Here in my cell, if I stand on the stool and peer through the bars of my high window, I can glimpse the marchers out in the street. A thousand strong, dressed in their Sunday best, they tramp there: wives, mothers, sisters, and daughters of the striking miners, still camped in their tent colony. How grand the marchers look — flushed, firm, their breath misting at their mouths.

They move as one, with the morning light on them: women in bonnets, in shawls, in long skirts, some in worn boots like mine. Fists punch the air as the marchers pass this infamous jail, condemned by the state as unfit for human habitation.

Now there's a surprise.

Maybe these women know of this, maybe they don't, but little it matters. I'm proud to see the spirit in them, the flame in their eyes.

"*Mother Jones Does Nothing We Wouldn't Do!*"

The signs are large, their words scrawled in charcoal. "Good on ya!" I shout, though no one can hear me.

"*We shall not be moved,*" the women are singing now. "*Just like a tree standing by the water, we shall not be moved!*"

"We shall not be moved," I join my voice to theirs.

Nine hundred striking miners have threatened to march on this town to free me. I fight the mist that fills my eyes when I hear first this — but I hope the men hold back for now. Led by a damn ruthless fool, one General Chase, the State militia is heavily armed. I hear all this from my jailors: a surprisingly talkative lot, they are, and grand fonts of information. They don't quite know what to make of this "white-haired pistol," as I seem to be called here.

I think these jailors like me, though, and that's a good thing. There's plenty who are not quite so kindly disposed. Every day now I receive more death threats: Crude drawings of my face, under a skull and crossbones. I'm keeping these drawings, every last one. If I'm turned loose, I could show them around at rallies and meetings.

Hell, I might use them to paper an outhouse.

Still the women tramp on down the street, lining out a new song:
"Solidarity forever...." Their voices brighten the chilly, still air.

Suddenly, then, I hear a different sound: this is not singing, not tramping boots. Scarcely breathing, I listen — and I know. This is what I have dreaded for months now: the clatter of horses' hooves and the shouts of soldiers. I whisper a curse as the cavalry nears and the women stop. General Chase waves his sword — and, abruptly, falls off his horse. The women burst into laughter. Chase reddens and scrambles to regain his dignity. I fear what else he might do to give a lick to his wounded pride.

"Disperse directly," he barks.

There is a silence; nobody moves.

"Be warned — Disperse now!"

The women hold their line.

"For the last time, ladies — Disperse."

The line does not break.

There is a moment of eerie stillness.

And then comes the one word order — to charge.

The street now becomes a sickening blur: The horsemen crash through the lines of unarmed women. I see a bonnet fly through the air, blue ribbons streaming. Swords glint in the light as they slice through the crowd. I watch a long blade strike a tall woman's head; her fair hair is suddenly drenched with dark blood. Horses whinny and trample and rear. An old woman falls on her face; a young woman's mouth frames a scream: "*Noooo*." And all the while, I am pounding my window with my two fists, and I cannot look, and cannot look away.

"Damn you to hell," I shout at the soldiers. "Shame to you—"

I break off as my jailors' gripping both my arms.

"Just talking to myself," I mutter. "Rare that it happens."

Firmly, they lift me down from the stool.

Outside, the screams and shouts are still rising. I close my eyes and wrap up in my shawl. I think of the Rathcormac Massacre, in another time, another place. Here, in this country, we thought that such things could never happen. We came here, in part, believing that dream.

Now, for my sake, thirty women are wounded — none killed, thank God. But what has been won? What has been lost? I hope that the marchers' spirits are angered, rather than dampened with regret. The schemer in me makes some quick calculations: the only gain would be good publicity for the strikers' cause.

This comes in quickly, just as I'd hoped. My jailor reports: The press slams the governor and his damned attack dog, General Chase. The violence is roundly and flatly condemned. Still, this report leaves me angry and saddened. I will hate the ring of those headlines forever. The newsmen have branded this disaster, "The Mother Jones Riot."

~~

I'm against violence.

I prefer drama.

Just now, I want to think of a different scene:

Bloodless, this one — with unlikely players.

Fifteen years ago, it was, but still fresh.

Fifteen years ago, come October.

As I write that word I still flinch.

October, October:

A black month, a haunted month, always, for me. Its days hold a lasting and unspeakable ache. Its nights bring the old dreams that shake me awake. I've shed superstitions I learned as a child, especially certain signs of bad luck: hats on the bed, gloves on the floor, ladders, cracked mirrors, birdsong after dark.

Still, I believe that October is unlucky for me — and not without reason, not without cause. I prepare for each autumn, starting in summer. I scout out difficult work to be done, and buy my train ticket early. I always like to immerse myself in others' struggles — and in the fall, I try damn hard to foster my own.

And so, in the autumn of '99, I took on a tough labor mission — the tougher the better, to my way of thinking. Again, I went off to the coal fields of west Pennsylvania, where I had worked for a decade or so, with some detours to mills in the South. I've organized women in Scranton's silk mills and I've been all over "anthracite country:"

mines in Mahoney Town and Shamokin, Ashland and Pottsville and Locust Gap. Sometimes, I've held union meetings in open fields and, often in the earlier years, I worked with others more seasoned than I. This time, though, I was on my own, facing a battle that was all but lost.

In the coal town of Arnot, the miners had been out on strike since the summer. Now, with foodstuffs low and winter at hand, the strikers were ready to cave in and quit. And who could blame them? They had gone up against a powerful company, one that owned them and worked them, almost like slaves. I swear, the bosses thought more of their mules than the lives of these men.

To keep them from joining the union, a straw-boss would send miners down into the most dangerous shafts, or into seams whose coal had worn out. With their small sons beside them, the men had "gone down the hole" sixteen hours a day, six days a week.

For their labor, they never received one crisp dollar bill. They were paid in "scrip" — worthless paper, except when it came to rent company shacks or buy goods at the company store or pay the fees of the company doctor. But mining ran deep through families, down generations, and somehow the miners wove songs from their struggles. I remember these songs, even now:

"Sixteen tons and what do you get?
Another day older and deeper in debt.
Saint Peter, don't you call be 'cause I can't go.
I owe my soul to the company store...."

I recall how I felt as I stepped off the train in the drab, weary town of Arnot, Pennsylvania, on what had been a sparkling fall day. I glanced up to see I the weather had changed. The weather held fair — it was only Arnot that had its own clouds.

Immediately, I felt an inner sinking. The skies seemed lower here and the air itself felt heavy on my shoulders. Even in sunlight, the dust-motes looked black. Tumbling leaves, like spills of gold coins, seemed to fall through a crack from some other world. In the distance, I could see women with buckets, listlessly picking over a dump.

Nearer, a striped cat sprawled, dead in the street, and past its corpse, a beer bottle rolled. As I walked on, the wooden sidewalk creaked underfoot. There was a smell of whiskey and urine and rot. Windows were shuttered or boarded up. Shop signs hung still, as if the town had ceased to breathe.

Ahead, to my right, on a long sagging bench, six gray-faced men had hunkered down. Their wool caps were threadbare, their flannel shirts worn. Pipe-smoke hovered about them like a damned soul. The men took my measure as I approached; I watched their mouths compress into thin lines. I guessed what they thought: They had mistaken me for a company lady.

Later, I learned, the mistaken clue was my flowered umbrella, neatly furled — I ditched it, that trip; never carry one since. In any case, there I stood, asking the men where lodgers stayed. They pondered this question in silent communion and then one man spat forcefully in the street. He met my gaze and pointed a few paces away.

I followed his finger to a three-story house, the color of ash. *Rooms To Let*, read a sign in its window. The shutters were crooked, as was the door, which opened a crack before I could knock. Someone surveyed me, then let me into the dingy front hall. The coat rack was empty, the gray shades were drawn. As I took a step, dust rose from the faded blue rug and more dust lay thick on a claw-footed sloping table.

I fought back a keen urge to cut and run.

Before me stood a wide-hipped woman with greasy fair hair and one blackened eye. Here was her price, she said: Three dollars a day, paid in advance, breakfast at six. I agreed readily — too readily, I realized; too late. The woman let loose with a flock of questions:

Where was I from?

Oh, all around.

How long would I stay?

Oh, for a while.

Did I know folks in town?

Oh no, not yet.

Was I looking for work?

Oh, maybe so.

Didn't I know, there was no work?

Oh, I'd heard otherwise.

The woman shoved her lamp close to my face.

Didn't I think that could burn someone's flesh?

Oh, I'd hope not.

Didn't I know, some folks burned in their beds?

Oh, no one's wanting such a dark thing.

What was I, Irish? A troublemaker?

An American citizen, proud of it, too.

Did I know the last fella here, a Mick, union scum?

I held her gaze and governed my tongue.

Did I know I gave the same answers the union Mick?

I spoke not a word, only turned toward the door.

And didn't he burn up one night in his bed?

As I went out, I felt the thrust of her boot in my back.

That night, I laughed with the miner who'd broken my fall as I'd lurched out the door, into the street. Getting kicked out had made me some friends; clearly now, I was on the right side. Big Black Bill Morgan had taken me in to stay with his family: Ada, his tall raw-boned wife, and their three children. Black Bill — so called for his dark Welsh looks — felt badly about steering me toward that boarding house.

"The company owns it." Ada ladled tomato soup into wood bowls. "And that Mrs. Clark, she's missing some screws."

"She seemed right daft — but this soup, it's grand, so."

"You're from Cork?"

"You can tell?"

"The Cork miners here always say 'grand, so.' "

"Ah. Are they still saying that, with the strike on?"

There was a pause.

"Them Cork boys is stubborn," Ada said at last.

"We'll be all right," Bill nodded then. "I built this lean-to."

"I grow tomatoes and beans," his wife added with pride.

"You can hold out, then?"

"Yes, Ma'am," they both said at once.

"Good. And the others?"

There was another pause, longer this time.

"More and more folks, now, they want to cave in."

"They figure they can't win no pay-raise," Ada put in.

"They're scared for their jobs." Black Bill looked down.

"I'm from the union," I said. "I think I can help."

Black Bill smoked his pipe, then passed it to his wife. She drew on it, exhaled, and handed the pipe over to me. Honored, I took a puff and tried not to cough. We sat in the circle of lamplight together, passing the pipe, and I felt an odd but powerful peace fold down over us.

In the glow of the lamp, I saw that the table and stools were handmade of wood. There was a shelf of pots and pans; a castor oil bottle held a yellow rose. Above the shelf there were tinted pictures of Christ, the Good Shepherd, and an angel with gilded wings.

Behind us, the children slept curled together on one straw mattress. That night, they shared it with their mother and me, while Black Bill slept at the table, his head bent, leaning on his crossed arms. As I drifted off, my mind filled with plans. In the morning, the Morgans would show me around, introduce me to folks. I'd try to start holding meetings and then try to get local farmers to help...

Dawn. And the sound of rough boots outside.

We all sat up, stunned.

The company's straw-boss kicked in the door.

"Get out, Morgan," he spat. "You and your damn union scum."

"I'm just a guest," I snapped back. "Let them be."

"Woman, shut up. Morgan, five minutes and you're outta here."

"We built this shed, it's our'n." Black Bill planted his feet.

"You deaf, boy? Get out or I'll torch every stick in the place."

The boss struck a match and laughed in Bill's face.

In silence, I helped the Morgans load their small cart with all that they owned: A ladle, a lamp, a mattress — a home. As we loaded the table, one leg broke off. That terrible snap set the children to wailing. And all the while, my mind was darting every which-way. My presence had brought on this shocking disaster — somehow, I must put it right. My thoughts rattled on, jumping from notion to notion. At last, I looked up.

"Listen," I whispered. "I think there's a way to turn this around."

The Morgan family just stared at me.

"I'll ask you to trust me — one more time." I lifted the last stool onto the cart. "What's there to lose? Climb on, Black Bill, and drive. Let your people see how bad you were wronged."

A long moment passed.

Forcefully, then, big Black Bill Morgan spat on the earth. He pulled the cart; we walked behind it. Slowly, we rolled through the strikers' camp. The children kept crying; folks came on the run. They followed us, passing the news of that eviction; everyone knew this could happen to them. We drove into town with a good crowd behind us. People stood gazing up at Morgan's cart. They scanned the whole scene: crying children; holy pictures wedged in with the three-legged table; pots and pans clanking; the splitting mattress, spilling its straw. And I remember that castor oil bottle, with its shedding rose. I watched the crowd: faces were flushed, fists were tightly clenched.

"Ain't right," a tall woman called out.

"Ain't right," the crowd echoed her.

I climbed up on the cart and lifted my voice.

"You see what your company men do for you?"

Something like a snarl rose from many throats.

"You think the boss gives a damn about you?"

The snarl turned into a low, deep growl.

"No — but you give a damn about one another."

"Right, sister," women called out. "We sure do."

"Then stand together and see this thing through."

I heard scattered cheers; the children stopped crying.

"Hell, don't quit now," Black Bill hissed at them.

They wailed at the scolding; I shouted again.

"Will you give in to thugs who rob children?"

"We won't!" People shouted.

"Can't hear you, say what?"

"*We Won't!*" The crowd raised a holler.

"Who will stand up?" I called. "Who will stand firm?"

"I will." Black Bill's big voice boomed. "But will y'all?"

"We will — yes! We will!" Fists punched the air.

I looked out at the street, now filled with people.

"Listen to this," I looked from face to face. "Out in Shamokin, a small town like this, the priest was giving a talk. He wouldn't let me into the church, so I held a meeting out in a field. The priest told striking miners — like you — "Obey your masters and go back on the job."

That way, he promised, when they died, they'd have a reward waiting in Heaven.

"The miners rose up and walked out and came to our meeting. I told them the same thing that I'm telling you: 'This strike was called so that you and your families can get some Heaven, *before* you die'"

A roar burst from the crowd and that roar grew.

Still, I knew, this was only a start.

I had to keep spirits high — and things could still go awry.

That happened faster than I'd expected.

Trouble rolled in with the train, the next day.

~~

Suddenly, they were there: Hired strikebreakers.

The company summoned them; now they'd hit town.

Scabs, we called them.

And other names.

Of course, we despised them. Wherever they went, they imported fear. They could make a strike break down pretty quick. Scabs took over strikers' work, for lower pay, and – so I've heard — those men were still able to sleep at night. I watched them slouching in Arnot's bars and swaggering up and down Arnot's main street. No doubt, Mrs. Clark's coat rack was full. I wondered how long it would take these "men" to get up the hill to the Dripmouth Mine.

"Good day, Ma'am," a scab tipped his cap as he passed me.

"Is it, now?" I resisted the urge to kick him in the shins.

If I felt that way, the strikers' would feel more furious still. They would want to break noses — and heads. Provoking fights was always part of the company's tactics. Then they could call in the law or get the state government all involved. Things could get ugly fast, but a brawl was the last thing this strike-zone needed. I had to figure a way to keep scabs out of the mines — without any bloodshed. I paced and I pondered. The strike had gone lame, so the governor had not called up the militia. Terrain here was hilly; no mounted thugs could ride anyone down. A strange idea came to me: it just might work, but there was danger to it, as well. I decided to test out my notion before I moved forward.

From shack to shack, I slipped through the camp to talk with the women of this mining community. At hearths and at stoves, I was heartily welcomed. From dented tin cups, I drank black coffee and listened to stories of struggle and survival. The words were plainspoken and matter-of-fact. Never did I hear a word of self-pity, even from widows. Every day, these hard-faced, strong women lived with one certain truth: Their men might never come home once again.

"We count on breakfast — not supper," a grandmother said.

"No fat hits the pan till I hear my man's step," a bride spoke.

Even so, these women swept floors and stitched clothes and stirred cauldrons of coal-blackened wash. They quilted. They gardened. They even laughed. And they sang proud songs of the mining tradition, passed down through the generations:

A miner's life is like a sailor's,
Aboard a ship to cross the waves.
Every day his life's in danger,
Still he ventures, being brave...

These were the mothers and sisters, daughters and wives, who stood firm on hardscrabble land in the hardest of times. Young and old, crones and brides, cooks and cleaners, they were all different — and yet, they were one. They decided my mind then and there. These were the people I needed to form a new kind of army.

To keep the women from danger, we moved from the firesides out to a field. There we stood in a circle and talked through our plans. We had to work fast, before the "scabbing" began. The last time I met with the women, the field was amber with clear autumn light, and the sun hung like a peach in the sky, and red maple leaves peppered the air. It was the kind of day when it seems that nothing could ever go wrong. I knew better. And this was October.

"I've told you the risks." I looked at them all. "No disgrace in walking away now. This is your tie to leave if you feel that's best for your families."

"We're with you," each one repeated, strong-voiced.

"I need to make a count: who stays, who goes?"

Around the circle, the women clasped hands.

Aside from that, nobody moved.

Just before sunrise, the "army" assembled in front of the mine.

The women took up their positions.

Their jaws were set, their hands were steady.

Each one was armed — with mops and brooms, pots, and pans, ladles and long-handled spoons. What a strange picture they made; that was for sure. They were plain and pretty, were heavy and thin, small-built and broad hipped. Their clothes were homespun purples and blues and calico. Their aprons were starched. They stood still and stood tall and they looked fierce. I stood back to gaze at them all:

An army of strong mining women makes a hell of a beautiful sight.

I scanned the line, seeking a leader. This was important. The best woman must be in charge; once the mine's entrance opened, I had to disappear fast. This time, I could not risk an arrest, which might lead to others. There was too much to do and I needed to stay close to the action. It took me only seconds to spot the right leader for this group.

She was a standout: Peg Sullivan, wed to a miner from County Cork. I supposed she had rushed to join the line-up — she looked as if she'd just rolled out of bed. Tall and imposing, she was still wearing her long thick nightgown. Over this she had pulled on a blood-colored petticoat, flaring out from her waist. One of her stockings was white, the other was black. Her head held a tangle of wild red curls; these sprung out in every direction, defying the bright, fringed shawl she'd tied over her head. Her face was flushed. Her blue eyes held just the right glint of madness. I looked her over and figured that this one could cause quite a rumpus. She nodded as I whispered instructions and she tucked her tobacco wad into her cheek. She was ready. As the sun began to appear up over the mountains, the whole stood ready, as well.

The mine's whistle blew.

Hidden behind a boulder, I watched.

The scabs, with their mules, were climbing the hill.

As they drew nearer, the scabs squinted ahead, then stared at the women. Startled, the men broke stride — then, dragging the mules, the scabs drew near. They stopped again, exchanging glances. No one had prepared them for this staunch line of hard-faced women. These women continued to block the entrance to the great Dripmouth Mine. I heard a light burst of nervous male laughter. That was short-lived. The women bristled. They literally dug in their heels and met the scabs with a powerful glare.

Confused, the scabs halted again. The women did not budge. For a moment, there was only the snap of the breeze and the snorts of the mules.

"What the hell—?" One scab blurted out.

"Is it hell you're wanting?" Peg's voice rang out.

And then, as if on signal, it began.

With a bone-chilling yowl, Peg smashed a clawed hammer against her tin dishpan. This she continued to beat like a drum. That crash alone was worth some white hairs, but the other women were joining in now. Pans became cymbals, clashing together; ladles and spoons smashed into pots. The ring of hills made every sound echo, twice as loud. The women set up an eerie yell, almost like keening, and thrust their brooms outward as if they were pikes.

The scabs appeared stunned. The company's mules, unnerved by this unearthly noise, skittered and tugged at their ropes. This in turn, pulled the scabs off-balance — and still, the women kept up their din. For nearly an hour, screams rose, pans clanged, and the men struggled to keep their hold of the mules.

Finally some of the scabs huddled together. I watched their lips and saw them form certain words I'd learned long before, on the streets of North Cork. One scab took a step toward Peg. She spat in his eye, and screeching, she went after him with her broom. As hell's furry came at him, the scab shook his head and stepped back.

"I don't do *this* kinda shit-work," he said to a comrade. "You?"

"Fuck it," his friend said. "Crazed women? Ain't worth my time."

They turned and left; others soon followed. The mine superintendent was called and came on the run, further upsetting the panicky mules. I held my breath; this was not part of the plan. I watched the boss-man: a young fellow, green. His hair was slicked back in company style and his trousers held a sharp crease. I had a notion that his starched shirt-collar might start to wilt.

"Shoo," he clapped his hands like a fool. "Shoo now."

"*Shoo*," the women hollered. "*You shoo now*."

"Stop this!" The man's skin was flushed. "Stop this at once."

"*Stop this*," the women screamed in his face.

"Quit it," he ordered. "Quit it right now."

"*Quit it right now*," the women shot yelled.

"Jesus, you hellions, you're scaring the mules."

"The mules?" Peg spat again. "The *mules*?"

"Shut up, you crazy bitch — move off that line."

"Bitch?" Peg's eyes narrowed. "You calling me 'bitch?'"

"That's right," said the super. "Now get your ass home."

"To hell with *you* — and to hell with your *mules*."

Rearing back, Peg cracked him over the head with her pan.

Stunned, the super fell over backwards. Before he could rise, the mules broke loose and charged down the hill. The chaos was a lovely thing to behold. It took hours for the remaining scabs to catch the spooked creatures, corral them and calm them. Meanwhile, the women's line held at the mine. By the time the light waned, most of the scabs had slipped off to the depot. The "Mop and Broom Army" had won the day.

That night, a new shift of women took over and thereafter, they patrolled the mouth of the Dripmouth Mine. It was tough duty, no doubt about it. The temperature dropped below zero at night and we were all living on dry bread and coffee. I'd watch with the women whenever I could. There they stood, an upended mop in one hand, and often, a bundled baby on the other arm.

Other nights, a miner's son drove me out to speak with the local farmers. The company had told them not to sell produce to the strikers, but as we sat and talked by the fire, there was a shift in the way those folks saw things. Often, when I drove the cart back from the farmlands, the boy was asleep on my shoulder, and over us hung winter's sharp stars. But the cart came back with butter and bacon, squashes and beans and milk in tall cans.

The strikers' spirits grew strong again. Led by Black Bill, they began to hold meetings, raising up other leaders amongst themselves. No scabs returned and soon after we rang in the new century, the strike was settled. The miner's got their hard-won pay raise — not nearly enough, of course, but a damn good start, we agreed.

Of course, the company differed with us. I was called a "foreign agitator," a title I've always prized. *The New York Times* condemned the tactics of "outsiders who arouse the miners' passions." I still have the clippings; I read them to remind myself what we did right.

One snowy night, the miners' families gathered with me in nearby Blosburg for a celebration. It was a grand evening — and our last one together. As I rose to go, a boy called out to me, "Mother, don't leave us." The children drew near — I took off so fast, no one knew why.

I picked up my bundle and boarded the train. In my satchel, I had stashed a first-class letter. It was from my own boss: John Mitchell, president of the United Mine Workers. He was sending me into a Maryland strike-zone. Meanwhile, he worried about my safety. There were reports that I was "raising hell with a bunch of wild women up in the mountains."

Had we been hurt? Mitchell asked.

On the train, I wrote back.

This time, I told him, we did the hurting.

It would not always go that way, I knew.

■

« 4 »

Now, one of my jailors has done the hurting.

He knows a few things about me, he says:

I'm the only woman who walks into mines and drinks with the boys.

I'm the only woman who walks into mills and brings in the unions.

I'm the only woman who's walked into this jail.

A dubious honor, I tell him.

You're famous, he crows.

He likes me too well, this tawny-haired boy with the broad shoulders, the gangly limbs, the careless tongue. He's only young, I remind myself. He doesn't know when to quit asking questions. To him, I'm some kind of celebrity; someone whose name often makes the papers. All his short life, this boy's heard about me — the stories, the tall tales, the news reports. Now he wants to know what's behind the tales and headlines. I can guess where his questions are leading and I do not want to follow him there.

"Were you always 'Mother Jones?'" he asks.

"Sure, I was born old, with a full head of white hair."

"You're a pistol," he laughs.

There is a pause.

"Got any family?" he asks, finally.

I stiffen in spite of myself.

"Some still in Ireland," I say — truthful but cold.

"Sisters and brothers?" he persists.

"Up in Toronto, where we first landed."

Another pause, longer this time; I brace myself.

"Children? A husband?" the boy asks then.

"No," I say, fast and sharp.

"But I heard–"

"You. Heard. Wrong."

Silence.

I feel stabbed; the boy looks stung.

Rescue comes in the form of a rat, circling the cell.

The jailor draws back as the rat sniffs his shoes.

"Big one," I comment. "Terrible long teeth."

The jailor stammers something and then he is gone.

My breath comes out in one long sigh.

"I owe you one, pal," I tell the rat.

Later that night, I am left to myself. There is only the lamplight; the scratch of my pen. I try to blot the jailor's words from my memory. *Got any family?* I print a date at the top of the page. *Children? A husband?* I stare at the paper; the date is all wrong. I must be losing my wits here, at last. The writing looks small and shaky, unlike my usual confident scrawl.

Were You Always Mother Jones? That question has never come at me before. I move from crisis to crisis; there's little time for probing the past. For decades, all over this country, I've traveled alone. People just seem to assume I'm a spinster. If need be, I mention that I used to teach; this serves to confirm the spinster impression. It's the rare school that will hire mothers. I rarely — if ever — fill in the gaps.

Now, I shake my head: an old trick I have for changing my thoughts. Sometimes, it even works. Warily, now, I spread out to my smuggled map of America. I'd procured this early on, to keep the jail's walls from closing in. Hidden in my notebook, my prize remains folded until things get quiet — I open it out when that seems safe.

The map reminds me of all the places I've been — it makes them real to me, once again. Arizona: I see its cactus and copper mines. Milwaukee: I see that brewery strike we won there. I can run my hand all over West Virginia and recall the mountains I've climbed to get to the strike-zones. But tonight, my gaze is drawn somewhere else. It is one state I always pass over — where I never worked for organized labor. I look away from it; then I look back. My finger traces the line of the great Mississippi and stops on a riverside city in Tennessee.

Got any family?

My finger remains frozen on Memphis.

A fixed address. A real residence.

My first and last proper home on this whole map.

~~

"Pinch-Gut" was my life for nearly seven years.

This section of Memphis was named by its residents — the hungry working poor. The neighborhood, Ward 1, held many Irish immigrants, crowded together in tiny houses, strung along narrow streets. "Pinch" was much like North Cork — it had all the same sounds and smells and spirit. Folks looked out for each other and everyone knew everyone else. I was at ease on Winchester Street, in a small two-story house which seemed grand to me. There, I woke to street noise and church bells and an odd feeling: Happiness seemed too precious a name. The times were turbulent, but they never pierced my contentment — until that seventh October.

Before then, I was frankly over-the-moon, absorbed in my own busy household. At last, I dared think, I had found my place in this world. A young girl can be so sure, so fast. I was just twenty-two when I came to "Pinch" for a new job. Despite what I'd lived through in Ireland, I was still young, still green.

After emigrating with my parents, I'd become a school girl, studying for my teaching certificate. Wasn't I doing things the right way? Wasn't I safe here, at last? I did not believe that disaster could find me, once again. After all, this was a new land; this was the place where people made their own luck. Later, in Memphis, I did feel lucky and those years passed in a bright blur: I could not know how they would end.

On bad nights, I wished I'd never come to Memphis.

No place for an Irish-Catholic Northern girl, my brother wrote.

I wrote that my job offer as the best one I'd ever had.

Come back to Toronto, my father wrote. There's talk of war.

I'll be fine, I scrawled back. Please, Da, don't fret.

You'll shame us, trotting about on your own: my brother again.

I never answered that letter at all.

My family had approved my first job: I taught at a convent school in Monroe, Michigan, for eight dollars a week. This post was arranged through Mother Mary Joseph — a holy dragon – from our home parish. To hear her talk this was a grand opportunity. But after a month in Monroe, I chafed against a raft of rules and restrictions. I hated to be as strict as I was required to be; I refused to rap children's knuckles with rulers. After a year there, I quit — and my family reeled with shock.

That was the first time my brother, headed for seminary, wrote that I would shame them all. It wasn't the last such letter from Billy. I did not come home but moved on to Chicago; I was itching to see a great American city. For a time, my family stopped writing to me, but I stayed on in a boarding house, paying my way with work as a seamstress. I had a knack for it; Mam taught me this art quite well. Even so, she was horrified that I, as a single girl, was living on my own in that "den of iniquity."

To make peace, I sent out new inquiries for teaching positions — and wound up in Memphis. I stayed with a Catholic family in "Pinch" and taught school by day. By night, I attended secret meetings: Abolitionist rallies in a rundown church. Memphis was hardly a favorable town for the anti-slavery cause but the folks at those gatherings remained committed.

Like me, they were also committed to a new politician from Illinois: an odd gawky man, sad-faced and eloquent and strangely compelling. The year I arrived in "Pinch," Abraham Lincoln was elected President of my new country: The United States of America. I heard talk about civil war but I'd heard such talk so often from Michigan to Memphis I didn't trouble myself with it much then.

Meanwhile, I longed to explore this lively new city. My chances of this were just about nil. My landlord , a sour-faced man named McCarthy, saw his duty as my guardian. No doubt, he reported on me to Toronto. McCarthy looked as if he had a perpetual toothache; so did is wife, a dutiful matron who actually did knit mittens for Missionaries. The McCarthys forbade me to go very far, unescorted, and so I kept to "Pinch," my school and the meetings. I noticed the Quakers who always came to these gatherings — and I noticed the tall blue-eyed man who always took a seat near to me.

He watched me and I did not like to be watched.

I would glance to my left and he'd often be there, directly across that old church's aisle. Maybe thirty, he was, I guessed — then flushed. I hated to admit that I thought about him. I couldn't help noting that he was the best looking man in the room: dark, with a fine-chiseled profile and a strong chin. I also noted that he had broad shoulders and rough worker's hands. One night a month, I heard him say, he always went to his union hall. I'd notice when he was absent and I'd notice when he was there for the anti-slavery talks. Never did he speak at those meetings, though he listened intently — between sideways glances.

He watched me watch him.

I watched him watch me.

We went on that way for two or three months. I was shy; so was he, I discovered. I often wondered how I appeared to him. I wore colors then: blues, greens and lavender. My hair was copper-colored, drawn up properly. You're a fair sight, so watch yourself, Mam had told me before I left home. I'd followed her advice; I'd not yet had a fellow. But here was this fine-looking man, taking all of me in, from my high-button shoes to my flowered hats.

I've always had a fondness for hats and it pleased me to trim them myself. Around Christmastime, my first one in "Pinch," I took out the old hat I kept for holidays. Two years before, I'd decked it out with the purple silk flowers that I've always loved. I wore it to a meeting, that December, and as we adjourned, a deep voice sounded behind me.

"Pansies?"

I turned, confused.

"Pansies."

That was the first word George Jones spoke to me.

"On my hat, yes," I stammered as I stared up at him.

"A fine one, Miss." He was polite, not a bit fresh.

"Made it myself, the hat, mostly, that is." I babbled.

"Grew your own pansies, too, I expect."

"Oh no, they're silk, they—" I broke off, realizing the

joke.

"Walk you home, if I might?"

I nodded, speechless, by then.

He took my arm and that Saturday evening, he took it again.

~~

George Jones knew how to have a good time. This son of Welsh miners and iron-workers, he was a man of contradictions: bold and shy, moody and merry by turns. He said he'd been waiting for years to "cut loose" in the city; he had not wanted to do that alone. For eight years, he'd been on his own, since his father had died, after teaching George the craft of iron-molding. Now he was a master at this highly skilled trade. Despite his quiet pride in his position, I sensed that he was a bit lonely — and more than a bit ready to settle down.

A tight Welsh clan had raised him in Kentucky, but at thirteen, he'd left school and come with his father to Memphis, where George had apprenticed. He did not like to speak of his mother, who had died in childbirth; he did say that he missed a family's "circle," as he put it. But first, he was ready to go out on the town.

George showed me Memphis, as I'd never imagined it. He took me to Beale Street, where musicians played in the streets and coffee-houses and bars. I had my first beer in one of those bars, with George looking on, amused at the face I made. One Sunday, we went to the famed Memphis Cotton Exchange; the only day of the week it was still. Another evening, we went to a dance hall where we learned how to polka. I remember the feel of my small hand, completely enveloped in his.

Then he took me up on the bluffs overlooking the vast river. A chilly wind blew; I secretly blessed it as George wrapped me close in his long arms. I don't know how long we stood there like that. Later, he told me, he had not even noticed the wind.

On Christmas Eve, George stood outside my window and sang to me. McCarthy and his wife peeked through their curtains to stare at George, this fellow I'd been "walking out with, and right steady." This was what they told my parents, I was certain. I wondered if this scene would make the next letter: There in the street stood George, hatless, in a red muffler, lifting his fine baritone voice.

"On the first day of Christmas, my true love gave to me—

A partridge in a pear tree."

He drew one single pear from his coat and passed it to me through the window I'd opened. I took the pear in my hand.

"On the second day of Christmas, my true love gave to me—

Two turtledoves...."

He took two chicks out of his coat and handed them over.

"Get those birds out of the house," screeched Mrs. McCarthy.

George sang on, undaunted, producing sketches of hens and more birds — if he'd had three real live hens, I think the McCarthys would have had a joint fit.

"On the fifth day of Christmas, my true love gave to me—

Five...golden...rings."

He slid five curtain rings on my fingers and sang on.

I went outside to join him and others drifted near. By the time we had gone through all twelve verses of that Christmas carol, half of "Pinch" was out in the street. Someone passed steaming cider around, and someone else passed whiskey, and, in the end, even the McCarthys were passing out cinnamon sticks.

The next morning, outside my door, there was a hatbox.

I looked around the quiet street and there was George, half-hidden by an ivy-trimmed lamp-post. With the unopened hat box in hand, I beckoned to him. The McCarthys were quick to invite George in — they wanted to get a closer look at "Mary's fella," I well knew. We sat side by side, "my fella" and I, on the sagging green sofa. The McCarthys took chairs and waited to see what kind of gift would emerge from that box. I lifted the lid and gasped aloud.

The hatbox was filled to its rim with purple silk pansies.

Later, as we walked about "Pinch," I gave George the hatbox I'd secretly emptied while he, alone, chatted up the McCarthys.

He frowned at me, thinking that I was returning his gift.

"Go on," I said. "Open it."

George lifted the lid. There in the box was a man's worsted tweed cap. He turned it in his big hands for some time. I set the cap on his shock of black hair and whistled at him, as lads do for girls. I wondered if George would ever speak. I began to fear that he had somehow taken offense.

"Where are the pansies?" He asked after a while.

"Safe in my drawer."

"Where are the rings?"

"In my left pocket." I jingled them.

"Here — you need one more."

We stood in the pale winter sunlight and gazed at the shine of the band he slipped on my finger. It wasn't gold, it wasn't broad; it held no gem. But it was the grandest ring I'd ever seen. We walked all over "Pinch" that day, talking and planning. Without a word, we stopped in front of a small brick-faced house on Winchester Street. *For rent*, read the sign in its front window.

We looked at each other and George hoisted me high into the air. I was small as a child in his arms. Soon, George said, he'd have enough money to put toward the rent on that little house. I knew this was true — as a master iron-molder, he made a good wage: twenty dollars a week. And I could keep my teaching job for a while.

Come spring, George said, we would go on picnics together. Come summer, he would take me to play on a traveling "showboat." The McCarthys, I told him, would not approve in the least. George slowly turned the ring on my finger, and laughed in the long, low afternoon light. By the time we went to the showboat, George whispered, the McCarthys would not have a vote in the matter. He was right. That July, when we finally saw the riverboat show, we were newlyweds. George had rented that little house on Winchester Street, in the middle of "Pinch." We had moved in right after our simple marriage in January 1861 — and I was just starting our first baby.

Easy, it seems now, when I think back.

It wasn't quite that easy, that smooth, at the time.

There were my family's inevitable questions:

"Why didn't you tell us beforehand?" they demanded.

"We wrote you, but the war's slowed down the post."

"Who is this George Jones? Who are his people?"

"Welsh iron-workers — immigrants like us."

"Mary, the Welsh are *not* at all like us."

"No matter, George was born in America."

"Why on earth did he go to Memphis?"

"Jobs, trade, the railroads — so much work."

"Mary, you're in a Confederate state."

"We got married before it seceded."

"This man, this George fellow, is he for the Union?"

"Of course — we met at an anti-slavery meeting."

"The McCarthys told us he sings in the street."

"I'm sure they did, they watched us closely."

And then the question I was most dreading:

"This George Jones — is he a Catholic?"

"He isn't. I am. Our children will be."

Silence.

No more letters.

I turned my attention to our new life and tried to forget:

I had no family now except George.

~~

Not for long.

I went into labor eight steps away from our front door.

Step one and two went quite smoothly. I counted the next six, since each one came harder, Still, I was determined to go out with George to the bluffs overlooking the Mississippi. The sky was already lit up by a naval battle there; canon fire seemed to shake Memphis as Union ships clashed with Confederate forces on the other side. General Grant had already surrounded the city, but blessedly, most of Memphis was spared any damage. Before Grant prevailed, I had begged George to take me with him that Sunday, although I was big by then, and somewhat unwieldy. Still, by my calculations, the baby was not due for a fortnight. Wrapped in a cloak to cover my "condition," I took my husband's arm and left the little house that we'd both come to love.

In our bedroom, upstairs, a wooden cradle was already waiting, with swaddling clothes that I'd made myself. Our house was a glory to me, tiny and sparsely furnished though it was. The whole place was spanking clean and dotted with blossoming flowerpots. I'd raised geraniums that first year, and wintered them carefully indoors. Every Wednesday and Saturday, the house was fragrant with my fresh baked bread. Homemade muslin curtains hung at our windows, where they turned pearly at dawn and amber at dusk. I'd hemmed our thin sheets and scoured our clothes on the fine washboard George had bought for me.

That washboard was a prize: not every household in "Pinch" could afford such a thing. Each evening, when George came home, there was some new thing to show him: A bedspread I'd finished, a cloth for the table — two brass candlesticks I'd pulled from a dustbin and rubbed to a shine. Outside, in our small bare plot, clothes flapped in the sun — blue and green and gold, they waved like small banners, I thought. My mouth full of clothespins, I hummed as I fastened each denim shirt to the line. Each shirt reminded me that I was now someone's wife. That was a great wonderment, to me. I'd always assumed that I'd be an old-maid school-marm, chained to a desk.

Now, every day, I made up our broad, soft, shared bed. One pillow held the imprint of my husband's dark head. Sometimes, I'd let myself think of the nights under those sheets, where George gently taught me what Mam never mentioned. Flushing, I'd hook my wicker basket over my arm and go daily to market. We couldn't afford much — but, after all, didn't I know ten ways to cook up potatoes? To go with them, I raised scallions, chives and leeks in a window box. Before starting dinner, I'd take old newspapers and wipe down the windows until they sparkled.

There was only one paper I never used on any window: *The Iron Molders International Journal*; it came every week from George's union. I missed reading and when I had time, I'd study the journal, I wanted to talk with George of his work for the *Union Iron Works and Machine Shop*. A huge place, it was, where engines were repaired, along with freight cars and grist mills. George worked there eleven hours a day and I wanted to know that other world he went off to each morning, six days a week. I had to admit to myself that I missed my husband while he was gone.

All of us women on Winchester street would hurry indoors just before dusk. Lamps would be lit and filled, their wicks well-trimmed, and before starting supper, I'd tidy the house, closing the curtains. For scent, I scattered clove-studded oranges all about.

Mam used to do that, I remembered. Often, as I went singing about my wifely work, I thought of her. She'd known how to tie curtains back with hair ribbons and how to iron starch into a shirt. From her I had learned how to embroider and kill a roach. The thimble I used every day was her gift to me when I left Toronto. Each time I brought a pot of water to boil, I recalled the day when she boiled the boots.

I tried not to think of my family's silence. The few letters I'd written them had come back, unopened. Slowly, I'd burned them all in the stove. Then I turned my mind to my new home and new husband — and the new baby, clearly on the way.

I remember how George's blue eyes crinkled up at the corners whenever he felt the baby kick. To my amazement, he even liked to look at the curve of my body. I'd tried to undress behind a screen, but every morning, he'd call me out into the light. I'd emerge shyly — I thought I looked like an overstuffed settee, but for some reason George thought I looked grand. He'd said that the boys at the iron works teased him for smiling, not only on breaks, but even as he bent toward the forge.

Still, he looked worried that day in June, 1862, as we left our home, and he kept a firm hand under my arm. In the distance, we heard the booming of cannon from the waterfront. I stopped walking. For a moment, I knew, George thought it was the gunfire that had startled me. Then he looked at my face, and the way I was wavering on my feet.

Never had I felt such sharp, twisting pain. I could not speak — I did not have to. George picked me up, big belly and all, and carried me back into the house. The pain let go then, for about twenty minutes; I could breathe once more. I climbed the rickety stairs on my own, though my husband remained close behind me.

"False alarm." My voice sounded queer.

The sky flashed; the house seemed to shake.

"Maybe not." George was watching me.

"Only a—" The pain clamped down again.

"Bed." George was firm.

In spite of myself, I cried out.

George wiped my face; I pressed his arm.

"Don't go anyplace." He tried to joke.

"Not...today...I...won't."

I heard his footfalls on the stairs. When he came back, the midwife was with him, and I was gripping the sides of the bed. I seemed to be filled with shattering glass. The pains were coming steadily now, every five minutes, then every two minutes.

George helped Mrs. Monaghan spread an oilcloth beneath me, to cover the bed. She poured a pitcher of water into a basin — and then she put a knife under the mattress. I'd seen this done many times back in Ireland, but George was horrified.

"What the hell—?"

"To cut the pain," the midwife explained.

George stared at her.

"Out with you," Mrs. M. ordered him. "No place for a man."

Ignoring her, he pulled up a stool and crouched by my head.

"Out with you now," the midwife repeated.

"I'm staying." He looked only at me.

Gasping, I nodded and clung to his hands.

"Don't you pass out, then," she snapped at him.

From the river, the great guns thundered on, covering my screams. Beads of sweat broke out over George's face. The midwife bent my knees and spread them apart. I remember her broad, flushed cheeks, steel-rimmed spectacles, her gray bun coming loose — little more.

"Babies come hard, the first time," she said, hours later.

"If I'd only known—" George broke off.

"Oh?" Mrs. M. glanced at him. "You'll change that tune."

The walls shook; the guns flashed. The room seemed to spin.

"Bear down," the midwife commanded at last.

With all my strength, I pushed through the pain.

"Good girl. Again. Harder — now, again."

Suddenly, there was a new cry in the room. The pain stopped. I saw George's eyes shift from me to slippery baby in the midwife's arms. I felt a tug, heard a snip, and the splashing of water from the basin. George's gaze had returned to my face.

"Mary? You all right?"

Still breathing hard, I nodded.

We looked at each other. There were no words.

As Grant took Memphis, our first child had been born.

~~

The year President Lincoln was shot, I gave birth again.

One month before Lee's surrender our son, Terence, slipped into the midwife's waiting hands.

Then on April fourteen, a great hush fell over Memphis; even the infant kept still in my arms. I tried to explain the news to Catherine, now three, and her sister, Elizabeth, only two. Kate and Lizzie, they were to us, both baptized in the new parish of St. Mary's. We went to Mass in an old school house while the church was being built, and there we gathered when we heard about the assassination. In silence, people came from all over "Pinch." It was such a fine April day, I remember; too fine, too fair. It didn't seem right to me, though I kept my thoughts — and my tears — to myself.

Every store and business closed down, including George's factory. We sat with our children and tried to find words to tell them what had happened. We wanted the children to understand that this was something sad and important — something we all must remember. Our daughters seemed to sense this through the city's deep stillness, and Kate listened solemnly to our words. How like her father she was, even at that age. Her eyes, dawn-blue like his, were fixed on me. She had George's firm jaw and thick black hair. What a beautiful woman she would become, I could not help thinking.

Lizzie was more like me: a redhead, freckled and small. A quick one, she was, and she learned to talk early. Her birthing was far easier than her older sister's, and Terence came so fast, the midwife nearly missed his arrival. He was a fine-looking boy from the first, and George thought Terence already resembled his own father, long dead.

My husband was pleased his son would carry his father's countenance, with his name, into the future. But George was proud of his daughters as well and when he could, on his way home, he would buy them ribbons and licorice. He was a tall enough man to toss them up to the ceiling, which always brought forth great shrieks of laughter.

I'd watch George gazing around the wooden table, as we came together for a lamplit supper. He'd been on his own so long, he did not take such evenings for granted. His joy in his family was a quiet thing, but I could see it in his strong face. Each birthing was always hard on him, though — even harder than it was on me, I believe. And each time, he swore, this was the last. The midwife laughed, as did I. George would keep to his vow for about six weeks, on average. And then, in our big bed, he'd reach for me once again.

He'd reach for me on other occasions, too, at a time when most men did not. George would take my hand on the street and kiss me out in the back lot, where neighbors could see. Everyone commented on us: Mary and George, still over-the-moon. Our household was noisy, crowded, and merry, despite all the usual tumbles and wails.

Sometimes, amid the usual clamor, I would recall my happy childhood summers with the Cotters in Inchigeelagh. And then I'd remember how abruptly the famine ended it all. At least once a week, I'd wake in the night and steal out of bed to check on our sleeping children. When I'd slip back to our bedroom, George would draw me into his arms and there I would drift back to sleep at last.

Now, the day of Lincoln's death, our house stayed oddly still.

Before we went to Mass, we tried again to talk to our girls.

"Remember the wake we went to?" George asked Kate.

"Mr. Murphy's." Kate had often played with his children.

"President Lincoln was a bit like Mr. Murphy."

"He had loads of children?"

"He had a whole country of children."

There was a silence while this was digested.

"But *you* won't die?" Kate's lips suddenly trembled.

"Of course not." George told her, quite firmly.

Kate and Lizzie ran to their father, clinging to him.

I still remember how they looked together, that day.

It's like a picture held in a locket: with me always, kept out of sight.

When George burned his hair, things started to change.

He came home one evening, his face scorched and his hair singed in front.

"My God," I stared while the children clambered about him. "What on earth—?"

"One fool stoked the forge too hot, too high."

"Can't the boss do something?"

"That fool's the boss's nephew."

"It still shouldn't happen," I flared up.

"It did. It will again." George touched his face.

"Can you get the boss to make things safe?"

"He doesn't give a goddamn about us."

George's laugh was bitter; I'd not heard that before.

"What can you do, then?" I pressed.

"Maybe my union can help." He didn't sound sure.

The lamps were lit and the wooden table was set for supper.

"Da, you look red," Lizzie observed after the blessing.

"Hsshhht," I said, as the baby started to wail.

"Could have been worse." George studied his hands.

"Worse?" I finished ladling out the stew.

There was a pause. My stomach turned over.

"I could have been blinded," George said finally.

A terrible silence came over the table.

"Eat, children." I had set down my own fork.

"Blinded?" Lizzie and Kate burst into tears; the baby screamed.

George, leaving his plate untouched, rose and slammed out.

"Where did he go?" Lizzie whimpered.

"His union hall," I said. Or a bar, I thought to myself.

We finished supper; George did not return.

"A story?" I asked the girls. "Or a song?"

Silence; then Terence wailed once again.

"Help me wash up, girls." I kept my voice bright.

A plate crashed to the floor and lay shattered there.

More tears, more wails. But no George.

I washed the dishes. I swept all the floors. I did the mending and sorted the wash. I went to the window a half-dozen times. When George finally came back, the children were asleep. I was waiting for him at the window, a lamp in my hand. He was unsteady and smelled like a brewery. Was this my husband, who always came directly home, who never went out drinking with the boys? I didn't know this new person before me. I didn't ask him where he had been.

For the first time, I was frightened; my small world was shaken. I took some cooking oil from the cupboard and offered to dab it onto George's face. He jerked away; then turned back to me. I went to him then, not knowing what else to do — all the while, wondering if he would push me from him. His arms came around me, though, and I don't know how long we stood there like that. In the end, we sat up in bed, talking and talking, as we'd done so often throughout our marriage. But never before about dangers at work.

George told me about the near-accidents he'd had at his factory. I'd never heard a word about them before. He was highly skilled, at the top of his craft, but because small shops had merged, forming big ones, he could never own his own place. He told me, with shame, that he did not even own his precious tools. George worked for the bosses of his factory and there was no getting around that — unless his union grew stronger. Above other trade guilds, the *International Iron Molders Union* was the most weighty, George said with some pride. And then he told me about the man who had organized it.

"Bill Sylvis says, 'Labor has no protection,'" George ran his big hand through his singed hair. "He says that the strong devour the weak. Most of the country's wealth belongs to only a few. That has to be wrong, Mary."

I remembered Ireland; I surely agreed.

"Sylvis believes that more money should go to the workers," George went on. "The bosses take more than their share and they don't better our working conditions.

But Bill Sylvis is out fighting for us. Most of us iron-molders belong to the union now. I get good pay because of union but—" He shook his head.

"Things need to change," I said. "I read your journal."

"The union wants a ten-hour workday, no longer than that."

I knew that George sometimes worked twelve hours a day.

"Will you get it?" I asked. "You surely deserve it."

"We might, darlin.' That bad war brought good times to us."

"But not good enough." I remembered the Journal's banner motto:

"Equal and exact justice to all men of whatever state or persuasion," I repeated what I'd read.

George looked pleased. "Sylvis, he speaks of labor's dignity."

"My father tried to get that for Irish farmers," I reminded him.

He nodded. "For my people in Wales, it was the same."

"Can Sylvis help you?" I heard the drive in my own voice.

"He says that if workers unite, they can help themselves."

"I'd like to meet this man — maybe someday."

"He wants to start a National Labor Union next."

The lamplight rippled across the bedroom's walls.

"I couldn't bear it if harm came to you," my voice cracked.

"I couldn't bear it if you had to take in wash."

I looked at the solid walls, the bedstead, and sighed.

"I won't take in wash if you won't burn your hair."

"Agreed?" George smiled for the first time that evening.

"Agreed." We shook on it before he blew out the lamp.

~~

Throughout the next year, George did more work for his union. It meant more nights out for him — and more time for me in with the children. Still I believed that George's efforts would pay off. I tried to savor all that we had. And at last came a great announcement: William Sylvis would soon visit Memphis; if we waited in line at the union hall, we might meet him. With George's co-workers, we were dizzy with the news.

It was almost as if the Pope was coming, the way we prepared for a handshake and a greeting. I trimmed George's hair and made him a new shirt. I refashioned a hat for myself; of course, it was decked out with George's silk pansies.

Maybe too many pansies, that time.

I pinched my cheeks to make them flush and fluttered about the mirror in the hall. Breathless, we asked a neighbor to watch the children. How do I look? we kept asking each other — and then there we were, in the shining great hall. Ahead was a tall man, a tree of a man, with riveting green eyes: I knew it could only be one person. "Himself," I whispered, as we approached.

"Mr. Sylvis, my wife, Mary Jones," George presented me.

"A pleasure," said Sylvis, shaking our hands.

"Mary's one of your finest supporters," George added.

"My husband is one of your finest members," I found my voice.

"You're the kind of couple I like to see," Sylvis looked us over.

"And you're a legend in our house," George said.

Everyone was so polite, I had to go and spoil it.

"What about women in unions?" I dared to ask. "A union should include women, blacks, immigrants—"

Someone stepped close and drew Sylvis away.

"Maybe I shouldn't have said that," I murmured to George.

"I think you should have." Sylvis was back for a moment.

We stared at him, a bit stunned; then we were all laughing.

"One day, George, you'll go on the road for the union, I hope."

"I'd be honored, sir."

"Jones — I'll remember that name."

And the great man was gone.

We were so excited, we went to a pub and drank to the union.

We drank to each other; we drank to Sylvis.

And then George made one more toast.

"To our future together."

I remember the clink of his glass against mine.

■

« 5 »

Inever read tea leaves. I never will.
Why did I let that neighbor read mine?
We sat in my kitchen, sun-splashed and calm.
"What can you see in that cup, Tess?" I laughed.
"It's nothing," she said, but her face had changed.
"What's nothing?" I watched her eyes waver.
"Dunno, can't see." She rose to go.
"I don't believe in it, Tess." I rose with her.
"Good. God bless, Mary." She was gone.
Our bright kitchen spread out around me.
It's nothing...nothing...
I shook my head and emptied our cups.
Can't See...God Bless.
"Nonsense," I muttered, suddenly chilled.

I began to get supper, lost in the chatter of children, the rattle of bowls, the smell of fresh bread. Outside, the air held the fragrance of flowers and garbage — common "Pinch" smells. As I pared potatoes and chopped green leeks, I rocked the cradle with one foot. By the time our fourth baby was born, just two months earlier, I had grown adept at cooking and rocking, all at one time. We had christened our newest child, Mary; George had insisted on naming her after me. In sleep, her small face was furled and flushed as a peony. She was a good baby; her cries were rare and she nursed well.

Lizzie, now four, took over the rocking, while Katie, a tall girl at five, stood on a stool to help peel the spuds. Both girl had braids, one dark and one fair, and I liked the shine of that hair; I brushed it each evening, with a touch of oil. Suddenly, at my hem, I heard a sudden clanging. Terence, just two, crowed as he rattled the pots and pans in a low cupboard. "Hsshht now," I said, for the twelfth time that day. I must remember to tie those cupboards shut, I reminded myself. Terence was an active, spirited boy. I never did know what he might bang up next. Even so my son's energy made me feel proud. His noise added to our home's distinctive music, as it seemed to me.

Soon the lamps would be lit and amber light would curl like cats on table and chairs. The house would take on its own warm glow, and into that glow, George would soon stride. Each day, I still waited to hear his step. So did the children, who rushed to their father well before I could free my hands. His face, every evening, was blackened with soot, but through it, I always saw his wide white grin.

That sweet June evening, George's step sounded slower as it approached. When he appeared in the doorway, there was no grin. The children did not seem to notice and, as always, he lifted them into the air. I wiped my hands on my apron and watched this homecoming. Something was different. The laughter was brief, the lifts were lower. Across the room, in spite of myself, I thought of the tea leaves and felt my back stiffen.

George washed his face and brushed my lips with his. Usually, he kissed me full on the mouth, in front of the children, and sometimes before he'd cleaned off the soot.

I often served supper with soot from his face, and his forge, on my cheeks. Supper, that night, was oddly subdued, though there was the regular chirp of small voices and once or twice, a whimper from the baby.

The clang of spoons against bowls seemed strangely loud and George was strangely silent and withdrawn. It wasn't until the children were sleeping that we climbed the stairs; he had something to tell me, he said. My heart was banging against my ribs as we climbed up onto our big bed. There, George took my hands and told me his news.

The iron molders' work had begun falling off. It had happened slowly but steadily, as things settled down, after the war. The small shops kept merging and the bigger business got, the workers' power — what little there was — had started to wane. It was an employers' market now. Workers were let go, some were locked out; some of the boys had deep wage-cuts. Listening, I began to feel chilled again. I feared what was coming — news that George had lost his own job. He was a master craftsman, I knew, and he had worked so long for his factory. I also knew good men had lost jobs.

"Tell me," I said and smoothed back his hair.

"It's not my job, darlin,' we still have that."

"Oh thank God." My words came in a rush.

"But hard times are coming."

"How hard?" I watched my husband's face.

"My boss layed off three men today."

I took a breath. "Old-timers like you?"

"These three were newer and younger."

"But you see more lay-offs coming?"

George nodded. "Another foundry just closed down."

"I thought we were in for boom times," I sighed.

"So did I, so did we all." George shook his head.

"The union—?"

"Losing members right and left."

"I *can* take in washing—"
"No." His voice was sharp. "We'll be fine."
"Sure, we've always been, haven't we?"
"That we have — that's my girl."
"Remember, I know how to boil shoes."
We laughed, then: thin laughter.
I did not mention tea leaves or Tess.

~~

The Devil's Bathtub:
   That's what some called Bayou Gayoso.
   Not really a bayou, it was a vast open cesspool. This swamp bounded "Pinch" on two sides and in summer we'd try to ignore the foul smell that Gayoso gave off. It was a fact of our lives and I rarely thought about it, except when the odor got bad. Then I would burn citron candles in the house and turn on our one ceiling fan.
   That summer of 1867, we had a long rainy season, and Gayoso flooded. When the rains let up, we suffered through hot humid days. I lit a lot of citron candles that August, until we ran out and could not afford anymore.
   It was still hot and went in September and the children fussed. George's step was slower as he came home from work. The heat of his forge was almost unbearable, I knew. It was bad enough in winter — that summer it was at its worst. He dared not complain — he needed that job. In the evenings, I'd wait for him with iced tea in my hand and he'd take it down in one long swallow. I worried about George but I knew he was strong. It was the children who concerned me the most.
   It began with red marks on their arms and legs. They constantly scratched at these mosquito bites, as everyone did, and I doused their skin with the calamine lotion that I loathed for its smell. One night, I felt a bite on George's arm and then one on mine. There were rumors of illness, but I felt sure I could keep my household healthy. I had lived through famine, emigration — and childbirth, four

times in six years. As a family, we had survived war, a race riot, and now, tough times. Whatever came next, I would fight it back. When it came to my family, I could be fierce.

Late that September, Kate ran to me; her nose gushed blood.

"Who hit you?" My voice was grim.

"No one, Mama. It just started bleeding."

"Just like that? Terence, too."

"When? Where is he?"

"Hiding. He didn't want you to see."

"Boys," I muttered. "Terry?"

When he appeared, I saw more blood.

I held their heads back against my shoulders. They bled through one handkerchief, each. I'd been hearing of nosebleeds from my neighbors, who thought this was an ominous sign. No one would say the dreaded words: "Yellow Fever." Nor would I, that muggy white-skied September day.

The children looked flushed and their foreheads were hot to my touch. Only the baby seemed to be cool. I put the others to bed, Lizzie included, who said that she ached all over. I sat with them, sang to them: I spooned broth into their slack mouths. The morning was warm but I felt chilled. I knew that with me, it wasn't fever. It was pure dread.

My children had always been healthy and strong; never before had I felt so helpless. I ran to the cupboard and grabbed a bottle of witch hazel. Making light chatter, I rubbed them all down. It seemed that years passed until George came home. There was no child to greet him, that night, at the door. He listened to the still house and looked at me.

"Thank God, Mary — you're not sick."

"The children, they're all down with something."

"I've heard bad rumors, two men were out."

"You all right, love?" I studied his face.

"Better be, I've got to work."

I saw then that his eyes were bloodshot.

"George," I said. "It just can't happen here."

He ate a bite of supper, then went straight to sleep.

I could not rest; I kept roving from bed to bed.

"Darlin',' sleep now," George spoke from the dark.

"For a minute." I lay down beside him and then it was dawn.

Mysteriously, everyone seemed to be feeling better. George, looking clear-eyed, went off to work. For the children, I cooked some oatmeal and it went down easily. Next, I gave them soda bread and strawberry jam; they seemed to enjoy both. I forced down some food myself, for the sake of the baby — I was still nursing. "Thank God, please God, oh God," I kept saying such words to myself. We'd had a brush with the Yellow Fever, perhaps, but it had passed off and now we were safe —"Please God," I said again.

Tess Doolin stopped by but did not come in. I shuddered at the sight of her, wrapped in her shawl in spite of the heat, her bulky body covered in black. She had one blue eye, one brown eye — a sign of "The Sight," she often remarked. Greasy white hair clung to her head. She made her living by stitching shrouds and telling fortunes. Her accuracy, George believed, came from her vast store of "Pinch" gossip. She eats it for breakfast, my husband would say. Now, like a great flapping bird, she'd come to roost at my door.

"There's sickness about, take care, Mary, dear."

"My children had a touch of it, but they're well now."

"Thanks be to God." Tess crossed herself.

"Yes, thanks be to God. How're you keeping?"

"Not too bad," she said. "Watch yourself now."

"We're grand, so," I said, fizzy with relief.

"May you stay that way," Tess flashed me a look.

"What's that you're saying, then?"
"After that first touch, it *seems* to lift."
"It," we both knew, meant Yellow Fever.
"I don't take your meaning, Tess."
"It can come back worse than before."
"No." My voice was fierce. "Not in this house."
"God keep you, then." She tramped off.
"And you." I slammed the door.
No wonder George called her the Angel of Death.

~~

When the first corpse appeared in our street, I knew "Pinch" was done.

Kate screamed as she looked at the body: a white man, fair-haired and still young, lying still where he'd fallen. His mouth was open; there was congealed blood on his lips. He must have been staggering out to get help. I hid my daughter's face in my apron. I didn't know what to say. If I told Kate the man was drunk or sleeping, my daughter would never trust me again. If I told her that plague was hitting the city, I'd frighten the child. In the end I said that a lot of people were sick, but it would soon pass.

I still could not speak the words, "Yellow Fever;" I still could not believe it would retreat, then return. The rich, we heard, were fleeing Memphis. The working poor, like ourselves, had to stay. Each day was worse, but my family held on. All around us, I could hear keening, mixed with shouts of delirium. Across the way, now, ten people lay sprawled, face-down. The city's death-carts would pick them up; only workers with permits could handle the victims. These were buried at night, with no ceremony. I believe they were thrown into mass graves, covered quickly with lime.

I closed the curtains. No one but George ventured outside, except when I had to go alone — to the market. I washed every bit of fresh food with great care; I boiled lavender to fragrance the house. Lavender, Mam always said, purified air. I thought of her as my own children looked to me for strength.

I tried to go calmly about daily tasks, enlisting my daughters to keep them busy. I swept, I cleaned, I sewed; I tried to sing. But all the while, I thought of the famine and every night, it filled my dreams. Once again, I saw green-mouthed corpses piled in the streets. George would wake me and hold me until I ceased trembling. My mind still held to that constant image: the grass-eating dead in the streets of North Cork.

Once, when I peered around the edge of the curtains, I saw Tess Doolin, her black shawl flapping, as she stepped over a corpse in her path. The sight of her gave me a shudder; before she could see me, I tried to draw back — not fast enough. "Ya can't shut it out, Mary Jones," she called out. "It's already in there." I hurried the children into the kitchen, away from the street.

"I *can* shut it out," I said aloud.

"Is she a witch?" Lizzie asked.

"Only crazy," I told her. "Crazy is all."

From Winchester Street, we heard grinding wheels.

"The death-cart," said Kate.

"Who'll help me bake?" I said brightly.

"Mama, let me." Lizzie came forward.

I stared at her nose; it was bleeding again.

Kate shrieked and ran to the mirror.

"Katie—?" I followed my daughter.

Her nose was bleeding, as well.

I felt my knees go weak on me then.

"Terence," I turned to him. "Come here to me."

"Mama?" he coughed, his gums oozing blood.

I snatched up the baby; she seemed to rights.

"To bed," I herded them up the rickety stairs.

"If we get sick—?" Kate looked up from her bed.

"Then you'll get better." My answer was firm.

The afternoon sunlight slanted across the room.
"No death-cart?" Lizzie whimpered.
"Never. People get well again, hear me now?"
People get well again, I told myself.
But I'd seen a yellow cast to the children's eyes.
"You're imagining it," George told me over supper.
"Look again." We sat at the table alone.
"People recover from this thing, you know."
"I'll see to that. You're all right?"
"Just aching from work, nothing more."
Again I felt watery at the knees.
"If anything happens to you—"
"Go to the union directly — they'll help."
"Don't talk that way, George."
"And claim my pension, that's first."
"Please stop this now."
"Darlin' Mary, stay well for me."
"We famine-Irish, we never get sick."
"Jesus, then don't. I couldn't stand it."
"If anything happened to you—" I said again.
"Nothing will." He lifted my chin. "Nothing at all."
"And the children?"
I could not look into his eyes.
"There's the real worry," he said, finally.
He took my hand and we sat there a while.
And then we heard the cries from upstairs.

~~

So began the week that divided my life.
It was the second day of October:
The twentieth anniversary of Gran Cotter's death.
I tried not to think of that as I tended the children.
All had been feverish throughout the night; George and I
took turns sitting with them, rubbing them down with
witch hazel again, forcing down broth and water and tea.
Around three o'clock, George fell asleep in his chair and I
led him to bed. As I walked him down the hall, I could

feel how heavy he was with exhaustion. I took off his boots and drew the sheet over his tall frame. I watched him for a while; his breathing was even and clear.

A false sense of relief came over me and I nodded off, waking when Terence cried out; he was having another bleed. Like all mothers, I'd sat up other nights with sick children — but that was different. That was measles and chicken pox – not the plague. No one knew what brought it on but there had been outbreaks in Memphis before, always after a rainy season.

Some of the old ones thought that mosquitoes carried this fever; others said it came from Bayou Gayoso. Everyone thought it was contagious and no one paid neighborhood visits just now. At least I would not see Tess at our door. I think if she came, I'd go after her with my broom.

At dawn, I splashed my face with water and wakened George.

Before he went out, we went room to room, bed to bed.

"Let them sleep," he whispered. "Sleep's the great healer."

"Take care of yourself, George Jones."

"Count on it." He kissed me full on the mouth and was gone.

I looked at the wooden beds, one a trundle, and up at the sloping roof, which had always leaned protectively over the children. It was the kind of room that always seems sunlit, the color of toast, the color of tea. Hundreds of bedtimes came crowding towards me. I could hear hundreds of stories I'd told in that room; hundreds of songs we'd all sung there, off-key. The room still looked peaceful — innocent of anything so dramatic and drastic as plague. That is the way I remember it, as it looked in those moments, just before the great change.

By mid-morning, Terence was awake and vomiting blood. His body was firey hot as I held his head over a basin. When he groaned, the sound tore through me. I wiped his mouth and looked at his face. There was no question now: his eyes and skin were not even sallow, they were the yellow of new wooden houses and freshly tanned leather. I held him against me and felt his heart beat against mine. His heartbeat was slower, then slower still. More blood oozed from his gums and he looked up at me, too weak now to cry. For a moment, I saw him as if I were gazing through a pane of glass — this could not be real. The glass seemed to shatter then, as Terence began a delirious chatter.

"Look, look, the horses." He murmured so softly I leaned near. "Blue horses, Mama, I want that one there — and the red one, can I have them? I need them to ride on, ride away, ride away, ride away now."

"You can have all the pretty horses," I remembered the song.

"Blue horses are biggest, I like them best."

"You'll have them, then, but don't go riding away."

He shook with a chill, I thought first; then his back arched.

"Terence," I called to him. "Terry, don't go."

His head jerked violently; I pressed him close.

In my arms, his entire body convulsed — then went still.

I carried him out of the room while the girls slept.

"Rest, child," I said. "The horses are here."

Then, on the kitchen floor, I washed his small body: his grandfather's namesake, his father's only son. I emptied a large crate of apples, lined it with a clean sheet, and lay Terence there. Upstairs I found the christening dress all our children had worn; it was far too small for a two-year-old boy, but I wanted to leave it with him. I rolled it up till it formed a pillow for his head. I dressed him in the shirt and short pants he wore to Mass.

I didn't want to lay him out in the front room before I told the girls. They were older, stronger; they would recover, I was sure. I didn't want them to scream at the sight of their baby brother, lying so still, there in a box. In the end, I carried the box up the stairs and set it in the room where I had birthed Terence. We had few candles; they were expensive. I lit just one, behind his head. The room smelled of tallow and apples and death. I tried to remember the right prayer.

"*Lux eterna...*" my voice cracked.

I glanced up, hoping that Terence would open his eyes.

"May light perpetual shine upon you—"

My voice broke again; I had to tell his sisters now. I stood by their door, preparing my words. Only words; no tears. Just the right words. I tried out so many, and still I could not seem to string them together. Instead, I went into the room where Terence had died, and I saw that I would not have to tell the girls anything for a while.

Both of them were tossing with fever; their eyes were closed and their faces were jaundiced. I leaned over to feel their heartbeats; these were still regular, fairly strong. I'd pull my girls through this — I swore; I prayed. I'd wake them soon and feed them strong broth; I'd set a lavender pot to boil in the corner. I'd sing to them and they could hold to my voice, like strong twine, and they would not let go. I was fierce as a wrestler, a boxer, a warrior queen. I put my hands on their hot foreheads and whispered one word, over and over:

"Live. Live. Live."

I nursed the baby while I sat with the girls. My namesake was hungry — she did not seem to be at all ill. Maybe my milk was keeping her strong. If only I could feed it to the others. I shook that thought out of my head and turned my mind to the hardest question: How would I ever tell George about Terence? There were no words for that, I was sure. Still, it would shock George if I simply led him up to the bedroom and showed him his son in that makeshift casket.

I thought about going up the hill to get the priest — we must have a Mass, we must have a wake. And all the while, I knew I could not leave. I could not even go to the market. Not with a baby, two daughters ill, and a dead child in the bedroom. This last seemed unreal; my eyes were stone-dry. I kept expecting Terence to call me. I listened for his voice throughout that long day, even as I fed the baby and forced warm broth into my daughters' mouths. They looked up at me with listless yellowed eyes and Lizzie whispered, then turned her head from the spoon.

"It's mother," I told them and waited.

They nodded; they knew me.

"Praise God," I murmured.

"Where's Da?" Kate asked me.

"Home soon, now sleep."

I left them to sit with my son.

By late afternoon, the candle burned down and the daylight was melting away. The house seemed to fill with rustling shadows. I rubbed my eyes; I'd gone notional for a moment. The girls were asleep; the baby slept, too, in the family cradle. I went about lighting the lamps — I always did this when dusk drew near and the air, for a moment, went violet-blue.

I could almost imagine this was like all the others: lamplit rooms, simmering pots, George's step at the door. This time yesterday, Terence had opened his blue eyes and looked into mine. I tried to shut every thought from my mind; there was a peace in this numbness — for a few moments. I waited for George, as I often did, with a lamp in my hand.

As soon as he'd closed the front door behind him, George paused and listened. The house was too still; I was too still. He could sense something amiss, I knew, though I could not read his face through the soot. His eyes held mine.

"What, Mary?" he asked then.

"The girls are fevered but holding their own."

"The baby?"

"She seems to rights."

"And Terence?"

I took a breath. "Gone," I said, weeping at last.

George held me till I could breathe once again.

"Did he go easy?" George's jaw clenched.

"Oh yes," I lied.

George followed me up the stairs and looked in on the girls. They opened their eyes when he called their names; they called out to him. I saw a wisp of a smile at his lips. He picked up the baby and studied her, then laid her back in her cradle. Then I took his hand and led him to our room. Stepping back, I let George have a few moments to be with his son. He gazed into the apple crate for a long while. Then he knelt by the bed; his shoulders were shaking. I put my hands on his shoulders and George turned his face into my apron.

We wept together till Lizzie cried out. There was a gurgling sound — I ran for another basin. We held her head as she threw up blood. Something like winter dampness came over me, though it was warm in this room. I could not tell George that Terence, too, had vomited blood before he had died. At last Lizzie sank back on her pillow, exhausted. I watched her sharp. She did not chatter, she did not convulse. George wiped her head; I fetched her broth. At last she slept quietly, as did her sister. We went downstairs in silence and I cut sandwiches for us; my hands seemed to move on their own. The kitchen sounds defied everything above us, on the next floor. We sat in the lamplight and talked for a moment: another warm day, we said. Would it rain? How odd, I thought — and how we needed that moment; that time out of time.

We could not bear to give Terence up to the death-carts, though that was the law. When it grew black-dark, George took out his shovel and spade. As I watched, he buried the apple crate in out tiny back lot, near its only tree: a maple, with leaves just edged with red. Each heave of the shovel seemed to release some sorrow in George. Together, hand over hand, we replaced the earth. It was hard to leave. We offered the prayers of committal and the Our Father. I left my grandmother's Rosary there on the grave.

~~

Dawn.

A peach-colored sky, a sudden breeze.

The curtains stirred as we watched Lizzie die.

George and I held her through the night through her convulsions. My husband, so stolid and strong, he kept whispering, "That's my girl, that's my girl." To the end, I think, we believed if we held her enough, if we loved her enough, if we prayed hard enough, she would pull through. Pictures tumbled through my mind: Lizzie as an infant, a bow holding up a thin wisp of hair. Lizzie, spitting oatmeal in my face. Lizzie, screaming with joy as her father tossed her into the air.

Elizabeth Ann: so like me in looks when I was a child, her coppery mane tossing on the breeze, gazing at trees she was too scared to climb. That girl with the fine voice rising in church, that child with the long, loving embraces — she could not be this yellow-faced creature, contorted, then quiet, drifting far away. Then came the gasping; we held her again. At last, as the sun spilled into the room, the curtains stirred and she breathed out, one last time.

"How can I go to work now?" George stared at me.

"For Lizzie," I said. "For the rest of us."

"Can you lay her out by yourself?"

I nodded. "I will. It's all right, love."

Why did I say that? Nothing was.

George staggered, I thought, as he tramped off. I ran after him; he'd forgotten his lunch pail. I didn't know if it was exhaustion or loss that had made him stumble there in the street. I dared not think that it could be something worse. After all, we were both stunned and lacked for sleep. Maybe today would be the turning point; maybe today, Kate would recover. Maybe this evening, we could start to mend.

I spent some time out back, beside the fresh grave. I found myself talking to Terence about big blue horses. I covered my mouth; the neighbors would hear and think me daft. Worse, they might tell the city officials that we had an illegal grave near our house. I went inside, fed the baby and looked in on Kate. Though her skin was still yellow, she looked serene, in a deep sleep. She did not seem to know I was there even as I touched her hot face with my lips.

Quietly, I washed Lizzie's body and dressed her in white: her church clothes. I seemed to stand outside of myself and watch this whole series of actions. Whose hands held the washrag — how could they be mine? How could this body be my own child? Again, a strange numbness covered me like a mist. I laid out my daughter and lit a fresh candle, set at her head.

Kate slept on and hung on — no bleeding, not a twitch. I sat there with the girls, as if they were both taking a nap. I could not comprehend the loss of two children in as many days. The morning went so smoothly. I ran out to market; there was nothing to eat in the house. I wanted a simple wake there for Lizzie; I wanted to feel normal for five minutes. I took the baby and the market basket and prayed that I would not run into Tess. I was not gone a quarter hour — but when I returned, there were police waiting at my door.

"Mrs. Jones? May we have a word?"
"Of course." I feared they would take Terence.
"You lost a child recently?"
I stared at him. How did he know?
"Mrs. Doolin reports that you did."
"Leave us in peace." My voice rose.
"I know how you feel—"
"You *don't* know how I feel," I snapped.
"We've come to collect the body, it's the law."
"Leave us alone," I was screaming by then.
"We have right to search the premises."
"Not on your life. Get off my stoop."
"I'll have to arrest you if you resist."
"Arrest me, then." I planted my feet.
"With a baby and other sick children at home?"
"Why can't you just let us be, for God's sake?"
"Plague victims go into designated ground."
"What kind of man can you be?"
"Open the door, Ma'am, no one wants no trouble."
Their boots sounded loud as they entered the house.
"My daughters are sleeping," I blocked the stairs.
"We'll see about that, Ma'am." They pushed me aside.
When they carried Lizzie down the steps, I must have
gone mad. I yelled at the police, I clung to my child. The
baby began to wail as I chased the officers into the street.
There the death-cart was waiting. Swiftly, efficiently, the
police wrapped Lizzie in a long winding sheet. I tried to
take her back; they pushed me away. I was still shouting,
as I heard the wheels turn and watched the cart go
"Lizzie!" I stood in the street, calling my daughter's
name. I don't know how long I stood there or who saw
me, nor did I care. Someone drew near; I spun around. It
was Mrs. Monaghan, the old midwife, who appeared out
of nowhere and led me into my house. After she shut the
door, I put my head down on the table and wept.

The midwife let me cry; she understood. Quickly and quietly, she calmed the baby, put up my groceries, and brewed us both a cup of strong tea. She said very little; I think she asked me if I took sugar. That day, I did. Mrs. Monaghan's presence alone seemed like a steady hand on my arm. I wiped my face and made myself drink.

"You'll have other children." The midwife gazed into her cup.

"But not these children." My eyes filled again.

"No, different children." She still stared into her tea.

"I don't know how to thank you for this," I said at last.

"No thanks needed, dearie." The midwife rose.

"Come back again, when things are to rights."

"Stay strong for your husband," she said at the door.

"So I will." I gave her my hand and my promise.

"And keep clear off Tess." She winked and was gone.

I went back to the kitchen and looked in her cup.

The tea leaves told me nothing.

What a blessing that turned out to be.

~~

We lost Katie around four, the next morning.

George and I held her, rocking her, as she slipped away. We never knew why she never went through the agonies of our other children; she only sank deeper and deeper into her sleep. Her face, so like George's, was a yellow mask as she lay on her back, her black hair fanned out over the pillow. Watching her, we still hoped that she would wake, healed by the rest. Then we noticed a change in her breathing; shallower, slower. For a few moments, her blue eyes opened. They were bright with fever but she looked as if she had returned to herself. We leaned closer. Kate looked at us and instantly knew us.

"Mama...Da...." Her speech was thick.

"You're our girl," George told her.

"I know." She gazed beyond the bed's foot .

"You'll be fine, Katie." I promised.

She still gazed at something we could not see.

"Look," she said then.

We followed her gaze and saw nothing.

"Bright, so bright." She smiled.

"It's all right, Katie, it's all right."

"I know," she said again. "Don't fret."

"Soon you'll be up and about."

"I'm coming," she called. "Coming now."

Once more, we followed her gaze.

At the end of the bed, we saw only shadows.

"Kate," George spoke sharply then. "*Katie.*"

I looked back at my daughter's face. A smile lingered at her mouth. Her eyes were open but glazed and unblinking — we knew that she saw nothing more. There was a new silence in the room; for a moment, I didn't know what it was. Then I realized what was missing: the sound of Kate's breathing had stopped. After a moment, George's big hand passed over her face and closed her eyes.

"There now," he said. "All over."

"You're sure?" I wouldn't believe it.

"Mary." He took my hands. "She's gone."

We sat with Kate until the sky lightened.

"You want me to stay?" He looked at me.

"What if you did?" I touched his face.

"I'd lose my job." His voice was grim.

"The boss wouldn't make allowances?"

"The union's not come that far yet."

George gave that short bitter laugh. We said nothing as he rose heavily to his feet. Slowly, like a man heading into a powerful wind, he went to the washstand. For a moment, he stared at it. Then he sharpened his razor and started to shave.

I watched his face in the mirror; what I saw there troubled me. He was only weary, I told myself — worn to the bone.

Sharply, I turned away.   Down in the kitchen, I
packed his lunch pail.   In silence, we went through the
usual series of gestures. Coffee was brewed. Bread was
toasted. Spoons clinked; the oven door groaned. These
everyday sounds seemed dreamlike and foreign.   How
many times had I heard George swipe his razor across the
leather strop? How many times had I heard my knife
thud on the cutting board? The ordinary had become
extraordinary; the familiar was strange. We moved as if
we were both underwater.

I shook my head and picked up the baby. She felt hot
to my touch; her mouth was too warm on my breast.   I
said nothing of this to my husband.   The man was
exhausted and weighted down with enough grief for one
day. I would pull this baby back from sickness while he
was gone. And I didn't want him to see Kate loaded onto
the death-cart. I was too stunned, too beaten, to fight off
city officials today.

At the door, George held me for a long while.

"You'll manage?" He said.

"We'll manage," I told him.

I lifted my chin as he went off.

"See you tonight," I called, as always.

"See you...." He lifted his hand.

After he'd gone, I wiped my wet face and went up the
stairs. I looked in the clothespress and took out Kate's
white Sunday dress.   She would have had her First
Communion just next year, when she turned six. I had
always imagined that she'd wear this dress. If Kate had
to go from me in the death-cart, she would go properly,
from her own mother's hand.

As I washed her, I wondered what she had seen at the
foot of the bed. Nothing, of course. She'd been delirious.
"Twas an angel," Gran Cotter would have said with
conviction.   I lacked such conviction; my faith was
nowhere near Gran's. Still, I wondered why Katie had

called out so clearly, so surely, "I'm coming." I hoped that she had more than shadows at the foot of her bed.

I slipped the white dress over her head and brushed her thick black hair, as I'd done so many times. By the time the death-cart stopped outside, Kate was dressed and wrapped in one of our own muslin sheets. I stared out the back window while the men tramped in and took her away. I said nothing, I tried to think nothing. Behind me, the front door slammed shut.

There was a pause; then I heard the cart creak as it rolled down the street. I turned from the window, smoothed back my hair — and threw up in the sink.

From her cradle, the baby cried out. I wiped my face and held that small bundle. The child still felt hot; her cries were weak.

"No," I said. "No, I won't let you go."

The baby whimpered.

I sat in the rocking chair where I'd nursed all my children. The floor creaked as we rocked together, two Marys, until we both drifted into a strange kind of twilight sleep. When I awoke, the light was shifting and changing like water across the room. I offered my breast to the baby but she turned away. I wiped the blood from her mouth and her nose before George came back.

What crazy notion had taken me? How could I hide this new outbreak from him? I took it into my head that my milk, with my own strength in it, could still cure this last child. I had not sickened; I seemed proof against plague. I prayed that I might the baby might draw strength and health from my own body. I moistened her lips with my own milk and turned to make supper.

When George came home, the lamps were lit, the baby was sleeping, and supper was waiting on the table. For about an hour, everything seemed to go on as always. Except for the silence. And the empty stools.

The high chair was gone; I'd dragged it out back. We passed the potatoes and spoke of the time we'd gone to the showboat, down on the levees. We had flown through the streets to the boat, I recalled, and the play made us laugh. George remembered singing out in the street, our first Christmas together.

We sat at the table and, like starving people, devoured good memories. We lingered there, enveloped in lamplight. That would become a memory, too.

■

« 6 »

I've never been good at talking to God.
That night, though, I cried out in prayer.
"How much more?" I raged at the Almighty.
I shut up the kitchen, slamming a drawer.
"No more, *No More* — please."
Silence.
Upstairs, George had fallen asleep.
I sighed and picked up the baby: still hot.
"*Hush little baby, don't say a word,*" I sang.
She whimpered and nuzzled my breast.
"*Papa's gonna buy you a mockingbird...*"
Weakly, the baby took in some milk.
"*And if that mockingbird don't sing...*"
More milk, more strength in that small mouth.
"*Papa's gonna buy you a diamond ring.*"
The milk came burbling back up, mixed with blood.
"*And if that diamond ring turns brass...*"
I tried again: If only she could keep down the milk.
"*Papa's gonna buy you a looking glass.*"
Again, the milk came back up.

"And if that looking glass gets broke..."
On my shoulder, the towel was soaked.
"Papa's gonna buy you—" I broke off.
I'd seen the yellow cast in the baby's eyes.
"Make it Stop," I implored God once again.
I felt helpless; no one seemed to be listening.

For most of that night, I rocked the baby and forced her to drink. I stubbornly held to my belief in the curative powers of mother's milk. It was all I had to give; this was all I could do. No one had any better suggestions. No doctor could stem Yellow Fever's course; no doctor or nurse would even come into "Pinch."

Damn them all, I muttered. I took it upon myself to save my last child — but even then, as I watched her yellowed face, I knew I could not. I wondered if I should wake George – should I spare him this sight or give him a chance to say goodbye?

At dinner, his eyes had been bloodshot; his face haggard. He had me worried; frightened in fact. How had he managed to work eleven hours a day throughout these losses? It was too much for any man, however strong. I decided to let him sleep on. In a whisper, I sang the mockingbird song again, then started on Christmas carols. Midnight passed. It was October fifth, I reminded myself. Somehow, each date seemed important.

The day before, The Feast of Saint Francis, I'd asked for mercy, for special protection, for grace. Of course, Francis blessed birds and animals — surely, he would include small children. The saint seemed to be otherwise engaged — how bitter it sounded; that voice in my head. I didn't know which saint ruled this day but the baby had lived to see it. Her gray eyes opened and looked up at me. Then her face contorted and her body shook. I held her tighter, rocking her through each convulsion. Another wave came, with a gurgle of blood. I rocked her and sang to her; she knew my voice. I was on the first verse of Joy To The World when I felt her go limp in my arms.

We buried Mary that night beside Terence. George hefted each shovel of earth with a kind of fury. I knelt by the milk crate where I'd laid out my namesake; she'd lived just six months. In the light of one lantern, we filled in the grave. It was so small, this did not take long.

When we went back in the house, I poured hot water over our hands and watched the dirt turn the basin dark brown. George seemed short of breath from his exertions; he sat at the table and buried his head in his folded arms. As if I were sleepwalking, I moved about. I put the kettle on and took out the butter, forgetting the bread. Maybe I really was asleep, I thought. If this were a dream, it would end and we could simply return to our life.

Thinking like this, I cut my finger as I sliced the soda-bread. I felt the sting of the knife blade and remembered: I was awake — this was unthinkable, but this was no dream. George woke to the sound of the kettle's whistle. For just a moment, I saw, he did not remember what had been lost. Sleep had rescued him for a few minutes. His face changed then, darkening. It was like watching a storm cross a lake. I poured the tea into our cups and sat down hard, weak in the knees. He reached for my hand; his own hand was hot.

"My God, Mary."

"I know."

"You all right?

"Yes, you?"

"I'll do."

We spoke like two people lost in the woods. There was no way to make sense of anything now. We did not try. The sound of keening rose from the house next door. All around us, we knew, our own scene played out in other kitchens. But there was no comfort, no answer in that.

We went up to bed. George could catch some more sleep before first light. But at first light, George could not get up. There was blood on his lips. I spread a wet cloth on his forehead and sent a neighbor's boy to the iron works. Again, blessed numbness enfolded me. I sat with my husband, watching him sleep, and when he woke, he drank my broth. He looked so strong, so big in the bed — I never thought the fever could beat him or take him away.

~~

For three days, time stopped.

It hung like a quilt set to dry in the sun.

How still it was, how heavy it felt.

"I'm all right," George said whenever he woke.

"Please God. Take some broth."

"Lord, no more broth."

"What would you have, then?"

"Apple pie. Hot. With cheddar cheese."

"I can bake one for you—"

"Truth: I couldn't eat it'"

"Tomorrow, you will."

"Yes, love, tomorrow."

At his bedside, I watched him breathe.

"I'm better," he told me on the second day.

"You're too strong for this," I quickly agreed.

In fact, he looked worse. I saw the telltale yellow cast in his eyes and the blood in his handkerchiefs — like a child, he had stuffed these under the mattress. This was only the crisis point in the fever, I told myself, and soon it would break. George was no child but a strapping big man; he needed rest, that was all. We were stunned, we were sleepless, and through it all, he'd worked at his forge — no wonder he had come down with this fever. I thought of the strength in his arms, in his back; surely that strength must outweigh this illness. He took some broth, then slept again.

Sometimes, when George was resting well, I'd go to stand in the children's room. The roof still sloped protectively over the beds. The light was still tawny and gentle and warm. There was a slice of blue sky in the window. At night, sometimes, the children would point to the moon, captured there. I looked in the clothespress and shut it abruptly. I could not yet face shifts and shoes. The room seemed to tremble before me — I pressed my hand to the wall to keep my balance.

The beds were stripped down to the thin mattress ticking; some day I should have burned the sheets that lay piled outside the back door. Were these the clues Tess had seen from the alley? Now, hundreds of "should haves" and "should nots" swarmed in my mind. I shouldn't have slapped Terence when he'd tormented that dog in the street. I should have paid more attention when Kate had prattled about her vivid dreams. I should have given more time to shy, timid Lizzie....this went on and on, until I left the room and returned to my husband.

"Don't go in there alone." George looked at me.

"I can't seem to help it, I don't know why."

"When I'm to rights, we'll go in together."

"When you're to rights, we'll do other things."

That night, I lit a lamp and did some mending, watching with George as he slept again. I studied the bed. There we had made ardent love so many times. There, I had come into my womanhood. There, all of our children had been born. Now, to my weary eyes, that bed seemed like a ship, swiftly bearing all this away. I shook that thought from my head and stitched up a rip in George's best shirt.

I could not remember how life had been before I was with him. The world had seemed colorless then, like a photograph before it's been tinted. *You'll have other children*, I remembered the old midwife's words. I took this to mean that George would not die; I knew I would never marry again. The lamplight flickered over his face, now sallow and spare. With all my strength, with all my soul, I willed him to live. "Burn down the house, turn my hair white, take all we own," I bargained with God — or was it the Devil? "Just don't take him."

That night, George was restless and weaker and warmer. Sweat streaked his face and darkened his nightshirt. I kept a damp cloth on his forehead and opened the window a crack. The cool October air seemed to soothe him. There were stars, I recall, and moonlight on the bedclothes. George opened his eyes and looked from me to the window

"Nights like this, we'd take walks..."

"...by the river," I finished for him.

"Then I'd carry you... back to this bed."

"How could I forget?" I took his hot hand.

"Don't," he said, fierce. "Promise, Mary."

"Never — you mustn't talk that way."

"It's time I did, darlin.'"

"No," I was frightened.

"Get word to the union."

"George, stop this now."

"*Promise*," he was fierce again.

"I promise," I said to calm him.

He held my hand in both of his and we had a few moments peace — suddenly, then, he staggered up and made for the basin. I held his head — there was blood. And more blood. George wavered on his feet and groped for the bedstead. If he fell, I knew I could not catch him or lift him. He leaned on me till he was back in the bed. There he lay, breathing hard, with a rasp to the sound. I got him to drink cool water; hot tea. I changed the sheet covering him and set a dry pillow under his head. Throughout that night, I held him close, till his sweat covered me, and his blood smeared my face. About five in the morning, he started to shiver; I held him fast, trying to take on the trembling, the fever, the sickness itself. His body began to twitch in my arms.

"Don't leave me," I whispered.

"Won't." He jerked the word out.

We clung to each other in that high bed until at last the room filled with pale light. George reached out to touch my face — his hand shook. I gripped it and he drifted back into deep sleep. I don't know how long we lay there before his breathing slowed; each breathe was a gasp. A dog barked from somewhere out in the alley. When the dog stopped, our bedroom was silent. I called George's name. I shook his shoulders and pressed my ear against his broad chest. His eyes were half-open. At last, I closed them, as he had closed Kate's.

~~

A man was rapping at the front door.

"Mrs. George Jones?" He took off his hat.

"You from the city?" I raised my broom.

The man drew back, sensing real fury.

"No, Ma'am — from the union."

I let him in and he took off his hat.

"We wanted to see how—"

He broke off when he saw my face.

"It was just this morning." My voice still shook.

"This morning." The man appeared to be startled himself.

The floor seemed to rock beneath my feet. There was a strange ringing in my ears. The room was beginning to fade and grow dark. The man led me to a chair and pushed my head down, between my knees. Light flooded back into the house and the floor stayed level; the ringing was gone. I was sorely disappointed. All I wanted to do was go back into the dark.

"I'd come to see if y'all needed anything."

"George said to send you word he was ill."

"The boys at the forge let us know."

There was a silence. My cheeks were wet.

"You'll need him buried," the man said at last.

The thought of the death-cart snapped me awake.

"Can you do the burying?" My eyes held his.

"We can and we will. We always do."

"I didn't know. Is there time for a wake?"

"Not now. We'll have to move fast."

"I'm grateful to you," I managed to say.

"We'll be back." He was gone.

"Sorry about the broom," I called after him.

I'd already washed George's body and dressed him in his Sunday best — his "wedding suit," as we always called it. After I'd lain beside him a while, I'd heard the death-cart out in the street. That got me up, preparing and scheming. I'd gone outside with one of his shirts and, singing and whistling, hung it on the line. "George," I'd called into the house. "I'll be getting your breakfast soon, love." My voice was so loud, half of "Pinch" must have heard me. It was a Sunday. Church bells were ringing. The plague was letting up; some folks were venturing out to Mass. I would not leave my husband. I went back upstairs and into our room.

George lay on our bed, surrounded by candles; I'd lit every one that remained in the house. A jug of wild flowers stood at his feet. The crucifix over our bed caught the light. The room was clean and the basin was washed. I sat with my husband and said the prayers of committal yet again. "*Lux eterna...*" I chanted softly and then there was only the buzz of a fly, the sputter of wicks, the drip of tallow.

When I heard a rap at the door, I glanced out the window. There was a wagon, just as promised. The International Iron-Molders, Local 66, stood at attention for a solid minute. These were great strapping men and I doubted that anyone would harass them. They covered George with a dark pall, laid him on a stretcher, and with dignity, carried him to the wagon. As they pulled away, I climbed on the wagon and so I was there as they buried my husband.

At the grave, the men stood at attention once more. They gave me George's union badge and said they would drape their charter in black for a month. I could not find words to thank them. Haltingly, I murmured that I'd always remember what they had done. They were all silent as they took me home.

The moment I opened the door, I listened for the children. I almost heard laughter, running steps, a baby's cry. The house was so silent, I wanted to scream. My heels clicked against the wooden floors — I'd never noticed that sound before. I went to the hall mirror. I took off my hat and hung it on the rack, next to George's tweed cap. I took off my gloves and laid them in the drawer. I took off my coat and put it in the clothespress.

Each action seemed huge, intense, drawn out. I went back to the kitchen and looked at the table. It was just as George and I had left it, the last night we sat there: Two cups, two plates, two napkins, two knives and two fork, and assorted crumbs. I thought that perhaps I should clear the table.

Suddenly, I swept everything — plates, napkins, cups, cutlery — onto the floor. I left it there and ran up the stairs. In our bedroom, I took off my dress and my stays. In my shift, I fitted myself into the place where George had lain, and there I lay shivering; my eyes were stone-dry. The pain had gone too deep for tears.

~~

That night, I smashed nearly all of the china.

Slowly, deliberately, I dropped each plate on the floor and watched the white pieces shatter. The platter went next. Then the bowls. My fingers were bleeding; the floor was littered with crockery — I wouldn't be needing it anymore. All the while, a still, sane part of me stood back and watched, and it was this part of me that set a cup and a saucer aside. I hurled pots and pans against the wall.

We had a freestanding house, otherwise I'd have had the police down on me again. I thought of burning the sheets, then decided to wait until daylight. In the meantime, I broke mirrors — what more bad luck could come now? Finally, I began trembling all over, and the room wheeled around me again. I literally crawled up the stairs, step by step.

From the laundry basket, I snatched up one of George's shirts and put it on. It came down to my knees; little I cared. The shirt smelled of him and so did the bed, where I curled up again with my head on his pillow. I stared into the dark, summoning it, willing it to swallow me, too. My eyes closed but the dark did not take me as I wished. I sat alone, through more nights of grief, always ending with a restless sleep.

Each day, dawn touched the room with amber light. I reached for my husband — and then I'd remember. My face would be wet; I'd cried in these sleeps. Now I could not get out of bed; I could not move. No one would come to me, I knew that well. People were tending their own sick; washing their own dead. Other homes were as stricken as mine. In any case, few would come into a "plague house." I heard the death-cart's wheels grinding outside.

After it passed, I heard someone rapping again at my door. Whoever it was, they had the wrong house. The rapping continued. I peered out the window — there, at the door, was a small group of women. Slowly, I moved down the stairs. I intended to send them away in short order. When I opened the door, all of them blinked. I forgot I was still wearing my husband's shirt. My hair was half up, half down. My face was streaked with the tears and dust. I must have had a wild look in my eye. The women drew back — then one stepped forward.

"Mrs. Jones," the woman took my two hands in hers.

"What have I done now?" I stared at her.

"Your husband's brothers sent us today."

"No brothers." The light hurt my eyes.

"Our men are brothers; they're in his union."

"And you —?" My voice shook.

"May we come in? I'm Annie Moore."

I stood aside, still stunned and confused.

"Our men thought you might need a hand."

"I'm grand, thank you." My voice shook.

The women ignored my refusals of help. They swept up the kitchen and found my clothes. The tea kettle sang from the stove once again. Annie Moore brought me tea in my only cup. The surviving saucer held chocolate biscuits: a surprise I'd been hoarding.

"I bought those for the children," I blurted out.

"We heard about the passings." Annie's brown eyes held mine.

"George said—" I choked on tea and tears.

Throughout that morning, the women sat with me. Annie Moore's dark head tilted toward me.

"Come with us tomorrow," she said. "Get out of the house."

They had a permit to nurse the sick. It seemed the last thing someone in my situation would do. I agreed to come with them, anyway. I felt I owed a great deal to George's union; a link with Local 66 was a link with him. I might as well help others such as myself. And secretly, I must admit this sorry truth: I half-hoped that I'd catch the fever and die. Whatever the reasons, I got dressed the next morning. When Annie Moore rapped again on the door, I was ready.

For a week or so, we went out among the sick and suffering — and each yellowed face, each bleeding mouth, was my husband's; my daughters'; my son's. Bereaved women wept on my shoulder; I could tell them why I understood. As long as I was busy, I could forget a little. As long as Annie Moore was with me, I felt her strength.

But at night, I sat alone in the chair by the bed. I dreamed of George coming back through the door. Each night at six, I listened for his step and at bedtime, I stood sentry by the children's beds. The walls of this house seemed to press towards me. I'd been so happy here — now I only wanted to escape. I thought again of sending a letter off to Toronto. I even put pen to paper, then let them drop to the floor. I picked up a newspaper and read it through, then found I could remember very few words.

It was in the papers that I found this news: The plague had broken. "Pinch" was decimated, but people had resumed their lives once again.

And I?

I had no life to resume.

There were no more sick or bereaved needing my comfort. The union wives could not give all their time to me. They still had husbands and children to tend.

I had the cemetery.

There I went, every morning, to sit by George's grave. In the afternoons, I had some neighbors' calls of condolence — but then a child called or a husband came home. I never went out after dark and at night, I sat alone in the lamplight. I'd collected George's pension and some nights, I paid bills.

One night, I emptied the clothespress and packed everything up in brown paper, tied firmly with twine. I could scarcely breathe as I handled the shifts and shirts, the trousers, the shoes. I found a handkerchief stained with my husband's blood and a rag doll that I had made for my daughters. I found myself gasping. My heart raced, my palms went clammy. I put my head down on George's coat until the spell passed.

I did not sleep that night. One thought kept circling in my head: If I were to survive, I'd have to quit Memphis. I penned a quick note to Annie at three in the morning. I had some clothing to donate, I wrote, and I needed to see her. She came right away. The union men's wives took the clothing away. Annie stayed while I set the kettle to boiling.

"We were so happy in this house," I began.

"That's all changed now." She was quick.

"I wonder why I didn't die with the rest."

"You wish it, don't you, Mary?"

I nodded, unable to speak.

"Of course you do." Anne was brisk.

I looked up, astonished. "You see that?"

"Yes...may I ask your intention?"

"I'm thinking I need to leave town."

"And do what?" Annie set down her cup.

"I'm a teacher.... a seamstress."

"My husband has a cousin in Chicago...."

"I lived there for a while." Our eyes met.

"She's a seamstress in need of a partner."

I hesitated. How could I leave?

"Think about it, Mary. It's a rare chance."

"I'll go," I said then. "How can I thank you?"

"Live," Annie Moore pressed my hands.

The next day, I went to the cemetery and sat for a time at George's grave. On my hand, two rings shone — the narrow one, for engagement, and the broad wedding band. These I would never take off, I told him. We would always be married; I'd never forget.

Then I went home and began packing. It didn't take long. I gave away all of my colored dresses. Everything black went into my bag. I donated my kitchen things, the rugs, the furniture, the lamps — nearly all that we'd owned — to Local 66. I swept the floor one last time. I dared not visit the graves in the yard, for fear I'd break down. I took up my bags and walked to the depot.

I left Memphis with thirty dollars and fifty silk petals.

■

October — again.

A black month, always, for me.

A hot one, it was, that year in Chicago. Its wooden buildings bleached in the sun; a drought had set in. I recall brown leaves in the parks and everywhere, pale parched ground. People were edgy; the murder rate rose. It was an ill wind that blew, some folks said. Three small fires had broken out that September, and the river ran low. I remember how the constant winds tugged at my hair and my skirts. Swirls of dust rose up from the streets, and the grit blew back in my face.

I felt a strong sense of dread, as if some storm were brewing — but I felt that way every October. I stifled this feeling every morning, as I walked from my rented room on Jackson to Washington Street, a few blocks away. There was the dressmaking shop I shared with Meg Moore and I kept a dress of green silk, displayed in the window. I was still in a haze, still stricken, even as I made that tribute to my heritage.

Teaching, for me, had been out of the question. I could not bear to be around children. There were many more things I could not bear to see: working men with blackened faces; young couples holding hands; family pews in Old Saint Mary's Church. Surely, I'd thought, I would feel better in this booming city; surely, I'd thought, I could outrun the past. This I was told and this I believed. For a short while.

Of course, as I quickly discovered, such notions are blarney; I might just as well believe that donkeys could fly —or horses were blue. *When you wake, you shall have all the pretty little horses...* I still wore my black clothes and dark hats. As I pinned up ladies' hems and stitched their lace collars, I always noticed the shine of George's rings on my left hand. I lived with a constant, sickening ache, but I never spoke of it, even to Meg: my kind, dark-eyed, quick-fingered partner.

We had luck with our trade, she and I. Ours was custom work and our small business flourished. I should have been pleased; I should have been thankful. Still, deep within me, that ache of grief remained. Through weeks, and then months, I stumbled, half-dazed and careless, except when I had a needle and thread in my hands. When I didn't, I paced the streets, staring blankly at the bright shop windows. I bought a narrow bed, a rocking chair, and a new rag rug. I thought they might cheer me; when that failed to happen, I bought pots of geraniums for my boarding house room. They were red, they were merry; they did not help me at all.

I realized that I was somehow trying to recreate our Winchester home. I broke into tears as I hung hand-sewn curtains, recalling how I'd sung at the same task in the Memphis house. When I made some more money, I purchased a pretty lamp, painted with roses. It cast a warm amber circle of light but the circle looked empty.

Faces were missing. Voices were missing. Laughter had become a novelty.

Most nights, I sat up alone, constantly sewing. As long as I kept my hands busy, I could get through each evening. I went to bed early and lay in the dark, longing for the touch of my husband's hands. Often, when I woke in the mornings, I could not recall where I was. I still reached for George; I still listened for the clamor of children. It was an effort to rise, brush out my hair, fasten my shoes. At my throat, I always wore the lace my husband had given me. My hats were trimmed with his purple silk petals. I kept to myself, ignoring the gazes of men on the street and in the neighborhood pub, where I sometimes treated myself to shepherd's pie and a beer.

"The first year is the hardest," Annie Moore wrote.

"Business is good," I wrote back; nothing more.

The second year, business was even better — but, to my surprise, I was not. I found that Christmas harder than the first; some of my blessed numbness was wearing off. Meg Moore invited me to her place for a holiday party; I could not decline. When I arrived in my usual black, a frown creased Meg's broad, freckled face. She offered me eggnog and, flushing, she introduced her new "beau." To this day, I cannot remember his name. There he stood, black-haired and blue eyed, tall and broad-shouldered. I murmured something and turned away fast. With a swish of her skirts, Meg followed me to the corner where I had retreated.

"Mary, it's Christmas — give us a smile?"

"I am smiling." This of course. was a flat-out lie.

"Burn those black dresses of yours, for God's sake."

"Now, Meg, you know I'm a widow."

"Time's passed, you're still young."

"I hope you're not suggesting—"

"You're one pretty woman – wake up, will ya?"

"It's a grand party." I tried hard to smile. Again, I tried to smile.

That next autumn, so dry and hot, I still wasn't smiling much, except when I put on a good face for fancy clientele. We were summoned to mansions along the north side of town; palatial homes strung out along Prairie Avenue and Lake Michigan. On rare evenings out, I'd visit my fellow immigrants and former neighbors: Cate and Patrick O'Leary from Inchigeelagh. Their part of town was nothing like Prairie Avenue, to say the least.

The O'Learys lived on DeKoven Street, about twelve blocks from my place. Near the railroad tracks, this neighborhood was crowded and shabby, crammed with immigrant Irish; it was much like "Pinch" and North Cork. By contrast, Chicago's aristocrats moved through grand, high-ceilinged rooms. I had many chances to observe their luxurious lives — Meg and I benefitted from their extravagance, I well knew. Each week, it seemed, there were parties and balls, and each week Chicago's fine ladies required new gowns.

I knelt on plush carpet to do countless fittings. I sat on overstuffed sofas in these ladies' homes, where I would sew on demand; I learned to run up a gown in a day. Often, I'd look though the plate glass windows and see poor folk outside these houses: shivering families, jobless and hungry, trudging along the frozen lake front in winter.

My own famine years would flash through my mind, as well as the recent season of plague, but I would stitch on, my mouth full of pins. I think those pins saved me from blurting out something reckless and harsh. In Memphis and Cork, I'd been able to keep to my own kind of folk, well within our own boundaries. Now I moved between two different worlds and these shifts were not easy for me. At least, for a short while, anger distracted me from my grief.

And so it went, until that next October, so hot, so dry, unlike any autumn I'd ever known. With the first of the month, I made myself busy. I remember I sewed six gowns in five days. There was a rush as Chicago's wealthy began their social season. The new luxury hotel, *The Palmer House*, had just opened to great fanfare. The Opera House had a spectacular opening, as well. The North Side ladies demanded new attire and I set about fulfilling their wishes. I remember that I worked late into the evening, on Saturday, October seventh; I cleaned up my shop on the worst day of all: Sunday, October eighth — the anniversary of George's death.

Exhausted and hot, I returned to my room well after sundown; even my fingers felt overheated. I took off my rings and doused myself with water from the pitcher on the dresser. Then I dressed, put on my hat and, for a bit of comfort, I went out to Egan's Pub, three blocks away. I sat at my usual table in the back, in the corner, and ordered a whiskey and a pork-chop, I remember. I rarely drank — this was a practice shunned by my parents. We had all seen too many Irish lives shattered by "a drop of the crature."

But every year after Memphis, I allowed myself one drink to blunt my memories. I nursed the whiskey and stared at the pork-chop before I forced it down. I was still stone cold sober. I was thinking of ordering another drink when a young man dashed into the pub, overturning a bar stool, and shouted, "*FIRE*!

~~

I remember this clearly:

People looked up but nobody moved. There was no sight of flames; no sound of a fire truck. Chicago just had a small fire, the day before; it was the third outbreak in as many weeks. The city's buildings were mostly wooden

and the wind was still high, the place was still parched.
Fire was not so surprising to any of us and that evening,
my thoughts were elsewhere.

Outside, the church bells rang nine-thirty; none of
them pealed out in alarm. Tim Egan drew a fresh round
of brew for another table. Hoisting a tray, a waiter
trudged by. I took a sip of my second whiskey and
contemplated the apple pie with cheddar cheese. I cut a
slice and gazed around the dim pub. Its windows were
shuttered, its tables were full. There was the usual smell
of beer and cooking.

But now, I picked up a different, sharper smell. At
first I thought it was something burning back in the
kitchen. I looked for the young man who'd rushed in with
his warning. He was gone, but I could hear his voice as he
ran into the street, still shouting that one word: *"Fire."*

"If that's a stunt, this boy's in trouble," Egan snapped.

"No stunt, sir." The boy was back now, and
breathless.

"What then? Where's your damned fire?"

The boy jerked his head toward the street.

"You'll drive off my customers." Egan strode to the
door.

"Jay-sus," he gasped as he looked out.

That time some people rose to their feet.

"Pay your tabs if you leave," Egan shouted.

I opened the shutters of the nearest window. Outside,
there was a strange orange glare to the sky. Others were
opening shutters, and then the windows. We craned out
necks, looking out. There was a fire down toward
DeKoven Street, I guessed. That was just about where
the O'Leary house and barn stood; my first thought was
for their safety. Still, Chicago fires were frequent and
quickly put out. No one panicked, no one fled.

I finished my whiskey, as well as my pie. I opened my
purse and set my money down on the table. By that time,

I learned later, someone had pulled a fire alarm in a pharmacy. It was just past nine-thirty when the church bells began to peal again — and this time, they did not go silent. All through that terrible night, they rang out, though the sound grew thinner as churches, with most of the city, began to burn down.

Most of us ran out into the street, then stopped where we were. A firestorm, fed by high winds, was engulfing Chicago. Already, the flames had run through the poor streets, tightly packed with wooden buildings. Like falling stars, we saw hundreds of blazing brands blow through the air, moving northeast. When the fire lit up a tall church just west of the Chicago river, I knew that the flames would jump the water.

And so it did.

The river was breached and the blaze roared on, jumping from rooftop to rooftop, in a strange rippling dance. This was unlike any fire I'd seen — it grew like a thundercloud, blown by those high winds. I ran toward my shop on Washington Street but by the time I reached it, the area was blocked off.

Swiftly, the fire was surging this way; the winds rose higher. Still, I had to get into our shop and save what I could. My entire livelihood lay down that block: not only our Singer sewing machines — and yards and yards of watered silk and sleek satin, velvets and lace and peach-colored taffeta, fresh from the warehouse.

Until I fashioned the goods into gowns, I made a sizeable outlay for materials. My employers paid well and in timely fashion, but that would mean nothing if this material burned. How fragile, how flammable, it all was, as well. Determined, I tried to slip through the police line. I looked respectable enough; I was still wearing my hat, for God's sake.

"Hold it right there," an officer's hand fell on my arm.

"I'm no thief." I shook him off. "That's my shop there."

"No one's allowed in no building down here."

"I just have to empty my place out, you see."

"I see that you're not going nowhere," he said.

"Officer, that shop there, it's all that I have."

"Haven't I heard that ten times tonight?"

"Twenty times true, I'd guess. Let me through."

"No Ma'am, it's for your own protection, I can't."

"I don't need protecting — my shop does."

"Sure you'd be burning up in it, so."

"You're Irish?" I searched the officer's face.

"From Cork City, like yourself, I can tell."

"Then be a good brother and let me pass."

"It's a bad brother I'd be if I did, well you know.

"Just for a few minutes, let me slip by."

"Go home to your husband, girl."

"My husband—" My voice broke.

He saw my eyes fill; then he let me go.

Just as I ran toward the shop, it took flame. The fire had jumped to the roof and now, like blazing fingers, it reached down to the sign that read "Moore and Jones." Beneath it, the plate glass window cracked. For a moment, the flames caught the sheen of the green silk dress I'd set in the window. I'd made that gown with my father's Ribbonmen in my mind. Now the silk seemed to evaporate and beneath it the curvaceous dummy burned like a woman-shaped torch.

The window shattered; the shop groaned, as if in pain. I heard crashes within, as beams fell through the floor, and soon I could not see the shop any more: only a wall of bright orange flame. The police jerked me backwards, away from the scene. My eyes ran, my lungs felt burned, and I coughed. I watched as my business burned to the ground, charring the velvet, vaporizing the silk, melting down the sewing machines. I'd learned enough about forges and cast-iron to know these were gone.

I hoped Meg had not been trapped inside; I doubted it, but that fear remained. I turned away, too stunned to weep. In my right hand, I clutched my purse; I wiped soot from my face with the other hand. I paused. That hand felt strangely light.

"Oh my God." I stopped in the street.

"Watch yourself," someone shouted.

"My rings," I shouted back; no one heard.

I'd left them on the wash basin while I had bathed. Then, weary and distracted my memories, I'd gone off without them. They were still there, as was some money tucked under the mattress. I broke into a run once again, but my feet felt like bricks and my legs seemed too weak, too slow. I heard my own breathing, loud on the air, and I heard my voice muttering, "*NoNoNoNo.*"

As I neared Jackson, I saw the police — this street, too, was cordoned off. Again, I tried to slip past the officers; again, I was stopped.

"Officer, please let me through."

"Off-limits, this block, now stand back."

"I have to get into my place just a minute."

"Not tonight, lady," the officer growled.

"My rings, my money — " my voice rose.

"With all due respect, Madam — are you crazy?"

"Crazy? I damn well should be by now."

I looked up — the fire had got there ahead of me, leaping like a demon across the rooftops. As I stared down the street, I saw 174 Jackson Street vanish into the flames. I thought of my lamp, painted with roses; the rag rug, the rocker — how hard I had tried to make that room home. I imagined George's rings turning to liquid as the wash basin blew apart; I could almost hear the crackle of money, like tinder, under the flaming mattress on the bed. I don't know why I kept watching the street disappear. Stunned and stricken, I could not move.

Beside me, another woman stood by, as transfixed as I was. I recognized her dark hair and her hoop earrings — she was Maria from Italy; my neighbor who had lived down the hall. All of a sudden, twisting and writhing, she let out a scream and leapt into the air. Embers had fallen onto her clothes; a plume of flame rose up her back. I took off my shawl and wound it around her, swatting at her back, all the while. A sharp black smell rose from the shawl but Maria was not badly burned. "*Grazie, grazie,*" she kissed my hands. She returned my singed shawl and before I could speak, she'd run off. I knew I'd never see her again.

From the tower of Old Saint Mary's Church, I watched the fire take over the city. Chicago was bright as day, that night, and I could see the wooden planking of sidewalks give way. The sky had an eerie orange glow, lighting the business district as it burned — then *The Palmer House*, the Opera House, large stores, small shops; thousands of buildings — gone in just a few hours. Turning my head, I watched the lumberyards blaze up so fast, I flinched. Lincoln Park was untouched and swarming with people, but riverside ships burned at their docks. There was a strange majesty to this vast sea of flame. Its power awed me and terrified me, all at once.

The great fire refused to spare even the wealthy, as the finest mansions vanished now into a rippling, howling demonic fury. I counted about thirty-five blocks blazing a path from the Irish section to Fullerton Avenue on the northside. I turned again, just in time to spot City Hall turning into a hill of ribbon-like flames. I climbed down from the tower then, thinking the church might go up next.

As I reached the street's remains, I was instantly swept up in a great herd of people. They were walking so fast, I feared I'd be trampled if I could not keep up. The fire was at our backs now and panic was fueling this silent stampede. What a strange army, we made — silent, singed, saving what little we could, we marched on in silence; there was only the tramp of our feet and the sharp bark of scattered coughs. I knew where we were heading without being told — as one, we advanced toward the shore of Lake Michigan.

There, we all plunged into the water, up to our knees; some up to their waists. And there we stood, gasping, as we watched Chicago burn.

We stuck it out there through the hours after midnight. Some of the church bells continued to ring out the grim hours and news filtered down from the bank behind us: Bad news passed quickly, in snatches and spurts. Just north of the river, the fire had crippled the city's waterworks. Chicago's water supply was cut off and now there was no way to fight back the blaze.

The mayor had called on other cities to help and meanwhile, fearing more panic out in the streets, martial law was in force. Our eyes searched the hellish scene spread before us; I spotted some clear patches, with the new Water Tower still rising above them, but those places were few. I glanced back at all the silent figures standing so still in the lake all around me.

"Looks like the end of the world," a man spoke at last.

"The end of my world," someone sobbed.

"Why?" Beside me, a woman's voice rose.

"Drought, wood, wind," the man answered her.

"No — why?" She repeated. "Why go on?"

"Surely, your family—" The man spoke quickly.

"No family." The woman wavered on her feet.

"Then for God, your creator," the man boomed out.

The woman gave a bitter laugh and sank to her knees.

I helped the big-voiced man pull her up.

"I have no family, either," I whispered.

"Then why?" Her blue gaze held mine.

Lacking an answer, I put my arm around her.

"No." She shook me off and sank down again,

We pulled her back up but she knelt in the water.

I watched her gray hair unfurl and float on the lake.

"Just try to get through the night." I tried to lift her.

Face-down, she sank like a stone.

An hour later, the churchbells rang through the dark.

"Three o'clock," I said, just to hear my own voice.

No one replied. We stood there as if we were frozen in place. I could hear people breathing and the lake lapping around us and the roar of the fire up the embankment; that was all. Then there was another splash in the lake, a few yards away. I never knew if someone had fainted or if someone else had just given up. In my head, I kept hearing the drowned woman's question: "Why?" I suppose we all asked that as we stood through those hours, there in the water.

I still had no answers — for others; for myself. Why had I survived plague and famine and fire, while others had died? I did not believe that God sent such suffering upon us. Nor did I believe that God had some special purpose for me. Perhaps, this time, I would not survive. I wasn't as strong as I'd been before I'd lost my family. Some spark of inner life had dwindled until I wasn't sure I could find it again.

I tried not to think of my shop or my room, the rings or the money or George's prized Union card. Such thoughts only gave way to others: The "Pinch" house, the Cork cottage; all the faces gone from me now. I did not even know why I went on standing there, through that night. I could only come up with one simple reason:

I be damned before I'd die in Lake Michigan's mud.

■

« 8 »

Like ghosts, we slowly emerged from the water.

Hazy sunlight came through the smoke-filled sky. The fire was not done with us yet, but the damage showed up, harsh and clear, in the daylight. Everywhere, there were smoldering ruins and these would remain, I knew, for days to come. Hundreds of homeless people gathered in Lincoln Park or down by the lake. Some wandered aimlessly, as if they were lost. Dogs ran loose; babies cried. Now there came a babble of voices, and still the city burned, snapping timber and running riot through other streets. There were police everywhere, trying to stop scattered looting. I tramped on to see if there was anything left on Jackson Street: Nothing but wreckage was left.

The fire still burned; in certain places, its devastation showed up, harsh and clear, in the morning light. Everywhere, there were mounds of ashes and smoldering ruins. And still the fire danced on into new areas; ahead of me was smoke, snapping timber, and those undaunted flames.

An odd silence had spread from the lakefront, up into town. People who passed me looked lost, dazed and helpless. Their faces were blistered and scorched; their clothing was blackened with soot. I looked at my hands and touched my own face: my skin was blistered, my clothes were covered in soot; I looked just like the rest.

Something drove me on, though — I stepped over burned beams and shattered glass — walking, walking, until I reached Washington Street. Where my shop had stood, just yesterday, there was only a singed, roofless shell, filled with fallen beams. I could not even spy a dull gleam of iron from the melted sewing machines.

Drawing my shawl around me, I moved like a woman caught in a storm. Head down, plowing forward, I went on through my neighborhood. Or rather, what was left of that section of town. There were only a few blocks between Washington and Jackson, but there was so much debris in the way, it took me more than an hour to get from one street to the other. Once I had walked that same distance in ten minutes.

I looked for Egan's Pub: now only blackened timber remained. I imagined the glasses exploding in the heat; I wondered if the beer had boiled in its vats; I hoped that Tim Egan had escaped in time. I reached Jackson at last, hoping to sift through the rubble for my rings: a foolish thought. The place where I'd lived was a smoking wreckage, still giving off heat. I began to feel the beginnings of panic running through me, but I was still dazed — a blessing, indeed. I simply could not take what had happened.

Chicago looked like some kind of fiery planet — as I imagined a planet might look: barren yet blazing, brutally bright. Later, the newspapers reported figures that seemed unreal: Four miles and 2,000 acres of destruction. 1750 buildings burned down. 2000 lamposts gone. Twenty-two million dollars in damage. 90,000 people left homeless — myself among them. Even days later, when I stared at these numbers, I was unable to take them in.

Now, well into the second day of the fire, I could only digest certain small facts: The heat from the city was so powerful, my skirt and my shoes had dried in two hours. Tiny blisters covered the backs of my hands. There was a white band of skin on my naked ring finger. Again, I wondered about Meg but I did not know how to find her boyfriend's place. Her own lodging house had been leveled.

I thought of the O'Learys, bearing the blame of a whole city, and my feet began to tramp toward their home. To this day, I don't know what gave me the strength to keep walking. Perhaps it was simply fear: If I stopped, if I dropped, I might never be able to rise once again. I needed to find someone from the old world in this new one, seared and strange. And I had to know if the O'Learys had somehow survived.

I followed the blackened swath that the fire had cut through the city, block by block, until I came to the poor Irish section. I saw the steeple of Holy Family Catholic Church — the steeple still glinted in the hazy sun. As I drew closer, I saw that the church was whole and untouched. I came around a corner, breathless, afraid of what I might discover. But there, straight ahead, was the O'LEARY' small house and barn. I trudged forward, calling to them. I remembered them both as fair-haired and freckled, green-eyed and kind.

"Cate? Pat? Are you in there?"

"Who wants to know?" Came a voice at the door.

"It's only Mary Jones, remember me?"

"Jones? Sure, we don't know any Jones."

"Mary Harris, from Inchigeelagh, Cork."

"Harris?" The door opened a crack.

"Gran was a Cotter, we came each summer."

"Cotter?" Pat O'Leary drew me inside.

"How're ya keeping?" I lapsed into my brogue.

"Not well atall." Pat bolted the door behind me.

"And Cate?" I watched as she crept into the room.

"Here's Mary Harris to see ya." Pat's voice was strained.

"From Inchigeelagh." I pressed Cate's cold hands.

"We've had dozens of threats." Pat shook his head.

" 'Murderer,' they wrote on our door," Cate's voice shook.

"Sure, you've been through it, Mary." Pat looked me over.

"Sit yourself down," Cate said. "Have a cuppa with us."

Cate O'Leary was in her mid-forties, about ten years older than I. Spare and pale, she had the look of the Creedons, her people. She was known as a sharp one at market and a grand, open-hearted housekeeper, as well. I remembered her, looking so grown-up, those summers out in Cork's countryside. Cate was the talk of the place when she married Patrick — a member of the great O'Leary clan, descendants of chieftains and old Irish kings.

Besides that, I recalled, I'd envied Cate's bosom, and wondered, as girls do, if I'd ever have one. But that was before the famine took over. I believe that the newlyweds managed to get out of Ireland quite fast, surviving the infamous "coffin ships," and making their way to a new life in here. How cruel, I thought — they'd escaped one devastation, only to face this one.

~~

"Somehow, the way the winds shifted, our house was spared." Patrick ran his hand through his tawny hair. "And the parish, it was spared, too. That makes people even more suspicious. As if we would start such a terrible thing. As if we would let a cow kick over a lantern into the straw."

"How easy it is, pinning this thing on the Irish."

"Not the first time. Or the last." Patrick's jaw worked.

"How did it really happen, do you know?"

"I caught a lad with a candle, stealing milk from the barn."

"Ah," I said. And he ran off, dropping the light."

"I tried to put out the fire — no use." Patrick sighed.

"You did well, Pat. Never should you or Cate be blamed."

"Blame's all over town. Like you said, it falls on the Irish."

I sighed and saw that the both of them were studying me.

"I must look a fright." My hand went to my blistered face.

"How did you manage last night?" Cate poured the tea.

"I stood in the lake." I managed a laugh. "Grand, so."

"And your home, your shop?" Cate paused, spoons in hand.

I took a breath. "Gone," I said at last. "Nothing left."

"Don't say your money was under the mattress?"

I nodded and, in the silence, I drank down my tea.

"It's not your fault, it's well I know that," I told them. There was another silence, longer this time.

"You haven't eaten for hours," Cate said, finally.

The O'Learys set a fine meal before me: Fresh soda bread, sliced apples, and Colcannon, rich with potatoes and leeks in sweet cream. As the old song said, this dish was "like a picture in a dream." In a quavering voice, I repeated that verse and the O'Learys looked brighter —

for a minute, anyway. In our minds, we had briefly escaped to the enchanted summers of Inchideelagh.

Rudely, abruptly, shouts outside brought us back to Chicago. "Get out you Micks, take your damn cow" A shower of pebbles pelted the shuttered window. Cate — tall, lovely Cate — started to tremble. She drew back against her husband's big shoulder.

"She's taking it hard." Pat threw his arm around her.

"It will go hard with us," she said. "You'll see."

"Please God, I hope not. It's sure to blow over."

"And you, Mary dear?" Cate looked up at me.

"Oh, I'll be just..." The heartiness quit my voice.

"We heard about George," Pat said at last.

I nodded, speechless; tears ran down my face.

They offered two handkerchiefs; I wept through both.

"I'm sorry," I said, thick-voiced. "Thank you."

"It's nothing we've done," said Cate.

Something gleamed on the table before me.

"I have another.... It's to go on with."

I stared at the thimble she'd set by my hand.

~~

"To go on with," I repeated, as I left the O'LEARY.

God bless them, ever and always, I thought. As I'd risen from their table, I'd wavered on my feet. Pat had caught me and Cate had put me to bed for that day and night. After breakfast, when I left them, I was wearing fresh clothes and a fresh pair of shoes, outgrown by one of their daughters. I took a last look at their low-beamed home, fragrant with turf from the hearth, clean and serene. In my pocket was Cate's thimble, two needles and a spool of black thread.

I could knock on doors, now, seeking mending, they said. They felt badly, I knew, that they could not house me, themselves. All beds were taken. One of their sons had slept on the floor by the hearth while I'd rested on new-ironed sheets. Two of the O'Leary boys had come home with blackened eyes. They had jobs in the building trade, as luck would have it. And it was luck they'd all be needing.

"Be safe," I said to them. "Never goodbye."

"God keep you, Mary, you'll be in our prayers."

"And you in mine." I tried to smile.

As I walked away from their warm, a thousand such suppertimes crowded my mind. I shook my head and watched each step; the path was still strewn with beams and debris. I felt something strange strike my head, then my hands. For a moment, I did not trust my senses. I lifted my face and let the drops fall on my cheeks, my eyelashes, my open palms.

"Rain," strangers sang out to me.

"Thank God," others shouted.

I saw people kneeling on the ground

Later, I learned that the rain had begun as the faintest of drizzles during the night. By mid-morning, the drizzle grew heavier and came down steadily. For the next few hours, Chicago sizzled and sputtered and hissed as the fire sank low and finally went out. The city smelled scorched and smoke hung in the air but the winds were now calm.

As I noticed the still air, I found myself back in my old neighborhood — not knowing why I was there. It was too soon to sift through the rubble for my melted rings — and I well knew they would never be found. I could not find Meg. I could not find Egan. I passed silent people who stumbled along, their eyes glazed, as if they were lost. They nodded at me in some kind of odd recognition. I realized it then: I was one of them now. The rain was coming down harder; I had no idea where to go.

The tower of Old Saint Mary's came into view. I hesitated, then went inside the church. The stained glass windows were darkened with soot and the pews were crowded with people like me. Mostly, they huddled in pairs or small groups. A smell of damp clothes and sweat filled the place. Two women stood in the back of the church with a cauldron of soup. I'd been fed well and passed them by.

I genuflected and found a seat toward the back. Gazing down the nave, I saw that the altar linen was fresh and salt-white. Before each statue, banks of votive lights flickered. Over my head, the churchbells rang nine. Exactly forty-eight hours before, I was sitting in Tim Egan's pub. I'd eaten a pork chop, I remembered, as if this had happened ten years ago. I'd lingered at table, sipping whiskey and pondering pie. I would not allow my mind to go back farther than that.

Now, in the church pew, I sat firmly on top of my purse, wrapped myself up in the singed shawl, and drifted into a guarded sleep. I dreamed I was climbing the rocky hills of Inchigeelah, but this time, I was searching for someone. The hills faded out and in a vast open space, I saw the one figure I had sought: a tall man's silhouette, broad shoulders, arms wide. The light shifted and I recognized his ink-black hair. His blue eyes seemed to beckon me close. I reached out for him as he reached for me.

Suddenly, I was jostled awake; someone new had squeezed into the crowded pew. In its corner, I huddled alone and tried to go back into the dream. It had seemed so real, I felt it had actually happened, somehow — somewhere, far yet near. I closed my eyes but sleep eluded me. I sat up in the dim church, listening to the breathing and sighs of the people around me.

"George?" I whispered.

Someone down the pew moaned in his sleep.

"George?" I whispered again. "Are you here?"

"Off your rocker, girl?" An old woman hissed.

"Why shouldn't I be?" I hissed back.

Silence. And then, down the pew, a man began to sing.

"*On the first day of Christmas, my true love gave to me...*"

"Shut up, will ya?" Someone called out to him.

"*...a partridge in a pear tree....*"

"I told ya, shut your trap."

Warmth seeped into me, then.

I slept.

~~

Mornings can be hopeful or harsh.

Harsh was that next morning, for me: A Tuesday, it was; October the tenth: the official end of Chicago's great fire. Bells pealed once again, and help poured in from other cities — food, medicines, furniture, blankets. I huddled in one of those blankets in Old Saint Mary's Church. I was no longer dazed; no longer numb.

Gone was the comfort I'd felt in the night. Now I looked around me with a ruthless clarity. I stared at the other huddled figures in the pews and saw myself in each one of them. The full force of my situation bore down upon me. As I named my condition, the words sounded cruel or theatrical. Still, these were the simple facts of my life now:

I was homeless. Jobless. Destitute. Widowed and childless.

"*Why?*" That question returned and remained. "*Why go on?*"

As I joined a soup-line, those words repeated in my head.

"*To go on with,*" Cate had said when she gave me the thimble.

But how to go on? Beg door-to-door?

"*On the first day of Christmas, my true love gave to me....*"

Coincidence, I thought, that morning; maybe a dream.

"Move along, girl." The man behind me had a rough voice.

"Sorry," I moved on with the soup line. "Go ahead if you like."

"Ladies first." He touched his hat. "You'll get used to this."

The line snaked ahead. I stood in the church's shadows and watched tattered people hold out their bowls. Tonight, thousands of people would sleep in the parks and the churches and the lakefront — tonight, and for many nights still to come. And I would be one of them. As the man said, I would get used to this. Or not, I thought. No one could blame me for giving up. Who would ever notice? I could see no reason to go on now.

I broke out of line and climbed the church's open tower. From this vantage point, I had watched the city burn; now, just as clearly, I saw its devastation. In the distance the lake gleamed in the light. Again, I thought of the woman who had let go and slipped so willingly under its waters. Now, from this height, I, too, could easily slip; I could take a long fall; there was no one to stop me.

"Hey you," came a voice somewhere below me.

"Who's that?" I leaned from the tower.

"What the hell are you doing up there?"

"What the hell do you care?" I snapped back.

Now I spied a man on a ladder, washing the windows.

"I care if you're thinking to take a big dive."

"How long will you be?" I called to him.

"Days," he called back. "So you'd best come on down."

"Leave me alone." I could see the top of his dark head.

"No, Ma'am. Too many jumpers around town today."

"Tomorrow, then. Not as if anyone's waiting for me."

"I'll be here tomorrow." The workman chuckled.

"The next day. It's not as if anyone's waiting for me."

"Where's your man, your husband?"

"I...lost him." Suddenly my voice went quiet.

"Who was he?" The workman looked up.

Maybe it was the blue of his eyes. Maybe I was just tired.

"His name was George Jones...we had four children."

"Where are they now?" He climbed up a rung.

"You don't want to hear."

"I've got time." His rag rubbed the glass panes.

For some reason I told him — about the house on Winchester Street, and our life there, and how I'd met George in the first place. It felt strange but fine to speak of these times after such a long while. I went on about other things large and small: the suppers, the children, the deaths, and the union; "Pinch" and potatoes and Halloween pumpkins.

"Sorry," I said, finally. "I've prattled on far too long."

"Not atall. I see why you'd want to cash it all in."

"That's a relief — if I decide to do it, I mean."

"Thing is, if you go, who'll know about them?"

I had no words to answer that question.

"No one but you can remember them all."

His words touched me like a fresh breeze.

"Hey, you still up there?" The workman called.

"I'm coming down, I'd like to meet you."

I ran down the stairs but by then, he was gone.

That night, in the church pew, I stayed awake, wrapped in my shawl. I went through each word of that day's conversation. I didn't know why I'd opened my life to up to that workman; I didn't know if I'd ever do it again. Maybe I was losing my mind, after all, blathering on like that. Maybe I could only speak of such things to a stranger. Maybe I'd just needed to talk. In the end, the reasons did not count for much.

If you go, who'll know about them? I wondered if that really mattered — but our life had mattered a great deal to George. *No one but you can remember them all.* That was true, I saw now. As long as I lived, they were a part of me. So was Gran Cotter. And Richard Harris and his Ribbonmen. *Never forget*, Mam had told us, the day that she'd served us boiled shoes. *Don't forget*, George made me promise, that last night we'd sat together at table. If I leapt from the church tower, no one would bear George's name into the future. We had thought that would be for Terence to do. Things had gone a different way — a way I could understand now, as I sat in that pew, wrapped in my shawl.

From my purse, I took Cate's thimble and slipped it onto my finger. I still had it on as I woke the next morning, dappled with light from the newly cleaned windows. I rushed outside to find the window washer. Someone else had taken his place.

As I went off to seek sewing jobs, door-to-door, I searched the streets for that workman.

I still hope that I can find him again.

■

PART TWO

PROLOGUE

« 9 »

Walsenburg, Colorado, 1914.

My trial is set for one week from today.
    Here in this jail cell, my lawyer gives me counsel.
    "Do us a favor: Don't swear in the courtroom."
    "Damn it, why the hell shouldn't I?"
    My lawyer throws me a look and lets out a sigh.
    "Make it easy on yourself," he says, finally.
    "I've never done that, I won't start now."
    "Hey, I'm here to help you, remember?"
    I apologize for going cranky on him. Maybe I've been
locked up a bit too long. Maybe my old hatred of lawyers
takes over whenever I see one: even this nice young man
with the floppy brown hair and the canny gray eyes. He's
from the UMWA — the United Mine Workers of America,
more formally. I've been a paid organizer for this union
going on fifteen years now. I got hired on after we won
that "Mop and Broom" mining strike in Arnot, P.A. For
my first twelve months, I remember, I earned five
hundred dollars. It seemed like a mighty fortune to me.

I guess it still does, but clearly, I'm not in this line of work for the money.

Somewhere along the way, I've learned how to stir working folk into action. In my purse, I keep a few clippings of quotes. John Brophy, a UMWA officer says that I can carry an audience without getting shrill. In fact, when I get excited my voice drops a pitch and grows more intense. John's a fine boy — he says my devotion is tireless. But right now I am tired, clear to the bone. John says I'm fearless; I disregard personal danger.

Fearless? That's not hard to manage when you've survived the end of three worlds. As for disregarding personal danger – well, maybe that's good and maybe it's not. I've had the law down on me so many times, I can't count them all. I'm not exactly new to the courtroom, as this lawyer well knows. Now I need the union as much as it needs me. I don't fool myself. This trial could put me away for the rest of my life. My attorney predicts a long and difficult battle ahead.

"Damn it, I don't have time for that."

"I just told you not to swear." He sighs again.

"In the courtroom, you said." I wink at him, then.

"That's good, use that Irish humor of yours."

"I'll try to behave," I say dutifully.

My lawyer studies me and looks doubtful.

"Be eloquent," he advises. "That's your strong suit."

"The gift of the gab — hope I still have it."

"Ah, Mary, you could talk blood from a stone."

"Is that something you read in the papers?"

"All right," he admitted. "But I've heard you do it, too."

"Blood from a stone — my life's story."

"Use that." He rises to go. "Write it down."

Shaking hands like two men, I thank the attorney.

"You're a hell of a challenge." He grins suddenly.

"Do me a favor, don't swear in the courtroom."

We laugh; then he calls the guard to let him out.

The laughter fades when the lawyer leaves. It's as if someone has pulled down a shade and shut out the light. I did not mention to him that my son would be his age just about now. I did not say that I still miss my husband when I lie down at night. I did not confide that spring, here at last, always reminds me of my simple wedding. These are parts of my secret self, borne deep inside me, where no one can spy it. I notice it daily, though — funny how long-gone events can spring up more vividly than this morning's breakfast.

People think you forget and move on, but I never do. When I look in the glass to put up my hair, I can make out the two faces there. There she is, the young wife who peers through a crone's mask of wrinkles. Sponge-bathing here brings more disappointment. My body, once firm and curving has gone soft as bread dough.

And who would imagine that I still have stretch-marks? George always liked to see them; they made him proud. Maybe it's a mercy that he never saw me turn old. Usually, I'm too busy to think about aging or how I look. But this jail stay has got me thinking backwards and now I can't seem to stop.

Blood from a stone. Yes. That's my life.

So it was for me, after the Great Chicago Fire.

■

« 10 »

Maybe it started with soup and a ladle.

That October morning, when I awoke wearing the thimble, I rose from my pew in Old Saint Mary's Church. All around me, people were starting to murmur and stir. Through the windows, cobalt and crimson and golden light dappled the nave. I walked up the center aisle. With some hesitation, I neared the long table at the back of the church. Since the fire's third day, morning and evening, I'd watched parish ladies serve hundreds of people from this wobbly table.

I looked closer, then: it was no table at all, only long planks of wood set on sawhorses. I had been too dazed to see this before — just one day earlier, I had stood in the line back here, myself. It had moved slowly; clearly, the servers were overwhelmed. Now I noticed the women arriving to serve up the morning's fare. There were only two of them, one old, one young, to manage three cauldrons. These were brought in by two strong young men: the older woman's sons, I assumed. Watching those boys, I felt what Gran Cotter used to call "a heart-scald."

I glanced at the shine of my new thimble. I looked at the glow of the sparkling windows. I took a breath and turned toward the women.

"Need a hand?" I stepped forward.

"Two would be better." They looked relieved.

"Your name, Ma'am?" the older one asked.

"Mrs. George Jones." I sounded proud and pained.

"Well, Mrs. Jones, here's a ladle for you."

"And here's the priest," I squinted at the altar.

"Mass first, always," the old woman said.

Bells rang; I didn't know why my eyes filled.

"*Dominus vobiscum...*"

The ancient words rang through the nave.

"*Et cum spirito tuo....*"

Throughout the Mass, the tattered congregation was hushed and respectful. As one, we knelt for the Consecration. I crossed myself with one hand, while the other still held onto my purse and the ladle. After Mass, I stuffed my purse into my corset, lifted the ladle, and watched the line begin to move toward us. It snaked through the nave, up to the altar, and curved around the statue of the Blessed Virgin Mary. Her hands were open and outstretched as people shuffled past. I looked at the thin brew of vegetable soup rising before me — as I ladled it out, I thought of Mam ladling shoe leather. This thought got me through hundreds of servings. I turned my mind from my own kitchen and tried to meet everyone's eyes.

"Good morning," I began brightly.

"The hell it is," a man snarled.

I changed my wording: "There you are."

"Bless you," a woman murmured.

And so it went, that first morning: curses and blessings, sad eyes and red eyes and eyes that never met mine at all. I looked for Meg and the window washer and the man who'd said I'd get used to this life. None of them appeared, at least at my station. And then I had two stations — the younger woman felt faint and groped her way to a pew; she was expecting again, she said. Another silent "heart-scald" for me. Slowly, I came to expect this, especially when children held out their bowls. I steadied my hands and kept on with my ladle. Just as my back began aching, the morning was gone.

The bells rang for noon Mass and I took to the streets, knocking on doors, asking if anyone needed new clothes, or washing for old ones. I found one customer who wanted a laundress, not a skilled seamstress. I could not afford to be proud. With my sleeves rolled above my elbows, I scrubbed clothes on a strange washboard and tried not to think about Winchester Street.

To my surprise, I earned a whole dollar, which disappeared quickly into my purse. As dusk began to fall, I returned to the church and helped the women serve supper: more soup, this time flecked with chunks of bread. I ate what was left, then found my sleeping place at the end of a pew. There, exhausted, I fell into a deep, dreamless sleep.

This was my pattern then: Mornings and evenings, serving the soup; afternoons, laundry or sewing; nights in the pews of Old Saint Mary's Church. People staked out their own spots in those pews and kept to them fiercely. That was all right by me; at that point, I was just grateful to sleep indoors. I saw that I needed a shape for my days. This was the start of a shape and, in time with the church bells, I held to it, no matter what. Chicago was rebuilding itself, and as it did, I thought I could keep to my pattern, until I could rebuild, myself.

So I thought — but I thought wrong.

~~

SOUP KITCHENS CLOSED FOR THANKSGIVING!

At first, I thought that was just a bad joke.

When the headline ran twice, I knew it was true.

All over Chicago, food lines and shelters were shutting down. Most places ran out of soup and endurance around the same time. Certain parishioners wanted to fumigate their own churches. There were rumors about lice in the pews — and worse things than that. Still, winter drew near and with it, a cold snap. Leaves swirled down the raw rebuilt streets.

That wind off the lake could slice you in half. I heard about people with frostbite from sleeping outside in Lincoln Park. During those last days at Old Saint Mary's, we didn't talk much as we ladled the soup. The women knew of my situation but no one spoke about it, out of respect, I suppose. I dreaded begging for help and so I stayed silent. At the church, I got by on one meal a day. This helped me save a bit of money and make a bit more, between washing and sewing.

On the eve of Thanksgiving, as we finished off soup and bread, the older serving woman approached me. Her dark eyes and dark brows were a bit startling, beneath with her white hair. Mrs. Malone had a sharp tongue in her head and the way she frowned now, I wondered if I was in for a scolding.

"I don't mean to pry..." Mrs. Malone began.

"It's all right." I kneaded my back with my fist.

"If you need lodgings, I know of a place."

"I can't afford much," I had to admit.

"My cousin's boarding house, it's not..."

"Expensive?" I took the address she held out.

"I've never been there but it should do."

"I don't know what to say." I spoke finally.

"I don't know what to promise," said Mrs. Malone.

"I'd rent a broom closet now and be glad."

"You just might get something like that."

"Right you be," I thought, one hour later.

I'd found the address in a seedy part of town.

"What luck!" Mrs. Sullivan crowed. "One vacancy."

"Lucky indeed." I peered into the tiny room.

"Sure, it's right cozy," May Sullivan crooned.

"Grand, so." I looked beyond her ample bosom.

"You're from Cork." Her plucked brows lifted.

"I am, and yourself?" I handed over my rent.

"Where else? We're thick there, the Sullivans."

"So I recall. This room's good and clean."

"Here's your key, now tell me what you do."

"I work," I said. "I'm a seamstress by trade."

"And who puts that henna on your pretty hair?"

"No one." I was puzzled. "It's just...my hair."

"You keep your little secret, then." She winked.

"I don't have any secrets." A lie, I knew.

"Any gentleman callers?" May gave a coy laugh.

"Oh no, I'm a widow." I saw her rouged lips form a smile.

"Sure you are, dearie." She winked again and was gone.

That was a strange conversation, I thought.

I pondered it as I locked the door with my new brass key. No matter, I concluded. I could afford Mrs. Sullivan's rent, paid in advance by the day or the week. This fee included coffee and toast, downstairs every morning, six to nine. My room was up two flights of stairs, tucked under the eaves, and the bed took up most of the space. I found myself staring at the night stand's lamp: Its red fringed shade matched the spread on the bed. The pitcher and bowl on the washstand were pink as the face of a falling-down drunk.

There was no place for a chair or a clothespress. In fact, the only large thing in that room was a wall mirror, tall and wide, reflecting the bed. Avoiding the mirror, I checked for roaches — no sign of pests. I turned back the bedclothes to find crisp, fresh sheets. There was no sign of dust anywhere. I began to feel lucky, indeed. This lasted about twenty seconds or so.

Another glance up at the eaves was my great mistake. Abruptly, I thought of my children's room in the house on Winchester Street. I fought back a wave of nausea and sat down, hard, on the bed. The mattress was firm and the one window was clear. Gusts of leaves flapped by like flocks of frightened birds. I hung up my shawl and took off my shoes. I was safe. I was warm. I was fed. Tonight, I would sleep lying down for the first time in six weeks. I'd made it inside before Thanksgiving. These were reasons enough to be grateful.

I lit the bedside lamp; a red glow spread over the room. I decided to think of this as a firelight. In front of the lamp, I held up two things: Cate's thimble and, from my hat, George's silk pansies. As I turned these keepsakes in the light, an iron bedstead began to rap rhythmically against one wall. When it stopped, I heard a man's full-throated groan. Behind another wall, the same sounds arose.

All at once, I started to laugh. A serious church matron had, unwittingly, sent me here — to lodgings that seemed to favor the oldest profession. I laughed till I had to unlace my stays. From my bag, I pulled out a small flask of whiskey: a parting gift from a woman who'd shared my pew at Old Saint Mary's.

I took just one swig.

"Here's to you, Mrs. Malone."

~~

One thing was certain in my uncertain life:

This was one hell of a switch from the church.

Throughout the years, great changes had hit me head-on, without warning. I'd started to wonder – and not without reason — if God was cruel or indifferent to me. In time, I would come to alter my thinking. Meanwhile, that first night at Sullivan's, I began to suspect the

Almighty of having a grand sense of humor. My surroundings had been completely transformed — I'd gone from pews to prostitutes in short order. Not that I cared; not that I judged.

I was just grateful to have a clean room of my own. I heard a lot through May's thin walls, and I knew those girls worked hard for a living. When we passed on the stairs, they were always polite and never asked questions. With a swish of tight skirts and a whiff of cheap scent, they would wish me "Good Morning," and head for the coffee urn down in the parlor.

Sometimes, as we gulped down May's brew, we spoke of the weather, the fire, the city's new boom. Then I'd go out to sew for my clients; the girls would go back upstairs to theirs. At first, I wasn't quite sure where I had landed and I dared not ask. I could afford the place, that was what mattered. It was a base for my work as a seamstress. Back then, I had no reputation to protect. In all of Chicago, the O'LEARY alone knew I was alive.

Even so, I must admit to relief when I learned that May Sullivan wasn't a madam and my new address was not that of a brothel. The boarding house simply catered to a certain kind of short-term clientele. By the time I moved out, a year later, I think I had stayed longer than any one of May's lodgers. I kept to myself, avoiding her questions. She didn't know what to make of me, in my widow's garb, with contrary red hair. All I had to do was mention my friend, Mrs. Malone, and that would swiftly end most conversations.

Days, I was busy rebuilding my business, while Chicago rebuilt itself from the ground up.

Sullivan's neighborhood was one of those sections that had escaped the fire. Everywhere, beyond it, I heard the sound of hammering and smelled raw new wood. I stepped over shingles and beams as I visited new clients' homes. I always used Cate's thimble and soon I could purchase more needles and thread. It was a grand day when I bought a small pair of scissors. I'd wrap my tools in my shawl and set out early to work all over town — except where I saw those hated signs: *Irish Need Not Apply*.

Towards dusk, I'd go to a decent pub with low prices: "The Leprechaun," known to its customers as "The Lep." I'd sit in the back, in a corner, and eat scrambled eggs if my day's pay was low. If I could afford it, I'd have a slice of Shepherd's Pie, though I never dared ask about its composition. The pie was hot and filling and cheap: fine fare for me, along with a small glass of beer.

Every Saturday evening, I allowed myself one slice of the house apple pie, in honor of George's last request for food. I'd read through the papers and then it was back to Sullivan's. Then came the most grueling work I ever did — wading alone through those long nights.

I'd sit in the lamplight and listen to the rhythmic clap-clap of headboards against two of my walls. Then I would hear men's repeated and ecstatic cries. This went on, hour after hour, six nights a week. At first, I'd managed to ignore it all; I was so grateful for a place to stay.

After a while, though, I came to dread every evening. It wasn't the noise that upset me, nor was it some sense of prudery. I knew what caused my nightly torture: I'd known a passionate marriage bed once, and these sounds summoned my most intimate memories. I'd rush from them down to the parlor, but it was always smoky and crowded and after dark, the streets were not safe.

I'd go back upstairs and think of my husband — and one night, I remembered how we had met. It was at a meeting, after work. Then I recalled the nights George would go to his union hall. Maybe, as his widow, I could visit one here. If anyone knew where I might find a group of tradesmen in Chicago, the source would be close at hand, just down the stairs, in Sullivan's parlor.

The next morning, at the coffee urn, I approached a tall girl I'd met on the stairs. Buxom but slender, she looked exotic; her long dark hair fell to her waist. To her customers, she was Viveza from sunny Spain. To the rest of us, she was Viv from Akron, Ohio. I asked her if she knew of the local Iron Molders Union. I thought she would burst into gales of laughter but she kept her face. Viv from Ohio posed no questions and gave me an excellent set of directions.

That evening, after supper, I followed them to an old, fire-scorched church. I opened the heavy door and paused. There was a meeting in progress so I slipped into the shadows, near the row of confessionals. As the meeting went on, I realized that these men plied various trades. They were not all iron-molders and this was not like Local 66 back in Memphis.

I almost turned away, but I'd come this far; I might as well stay. Soon, I was caught up in the men's talk of wages and hours and workers' rights. I recalled how George and I met William Sylvis; I took a step closer. As I listened, I gleaned more facts: these men wanted to join a new, upcoming, national union, one that accepted all working folk, skilled and unskilled, native and immigrant, black and white.

I'd never heard of such an outlook before; I wanted to learn more about this organization. I did not realize it would be famous; the mother of all major unions to come. Nor could I guess that my future lay with it. That evening, all I knew was its ideals and its name – *The Knights of Labor*.

~~

Evenings were different for me, after that.

Still, I did not realize my whole life was turning in a new direction. These changes came so gradually and so obscurely, I scarcely noticed how deep they went. Nor did anyone else, for that matter. In Chicago, The Knights of

Labor was not yet an official organization. Even so, it had inspired small cells to meet quietly, wherever they could. I'd come upon one of the larger groups; it met every evening in that ruined church and I there I returned, again and again, right after supper. I stood in the nave's shadows for a while, unsure if these gatherings would welcome me.

One evening, there was a stir — an out-of-state visitor was coming to address the meeting. In the back of the church, I waited to see him arrive: a tall, reed-thin fellow with a long dropping moustache. He was one of those young intense men who looked weathered and older. I watched him stand up behind an upended crate, used for a podium. He scanned the place and took everything in.

"Greetings to you, gentlemen — and lady," he began.

Discovered, I stepped out of the shadows.

"Have a seat, Ma'am," said Terence Powderly.

I took a place in the back pew, I remember, and soon forgot myself as I listened to the stirring speech I heard that night. Powderly spoke to the skilled and unskilled workers with equal respect. He even addressed new immigrants — and did so without condescension.

"Educate yourselves, men; don't you know that's the key?" His gray eyes moved from face to face. "Organize, that comes first. You have the power to change your own condition. You'll get nowhere one by one — but stand together and you stand strong. The time is coming to confront your bosses. Do you think you deserve better working conditions?"

A murmur rose from the men in the church.

"Do you think working folk deserve dignity?"

A rumble resounded throughout the nave.

"Here in America, you all can have it."

Applauding, the audience rose as one.

"Work for it with me, reach for it now."

I was on my feet, cheering with the rest.

After the meeting, the men lined up to shake Powderly's hand. I hung back, but he beckoned me forward. I looked into his face but I could not yet speak. From his name and his looks, I knew that he, too, was an Irish-Catholic American. His parents were immigrants; he was born in Carbondale, Pennsylvania: a first-generation American. Powderly looked even younger up close, but he was gifted and on the rise.

By that time, I'd learned that William Sylvis's National Labor Union was failing. The Knights of Labor, led by Uriah Stephens, was gaining power. And so was young Terence Powderly, Stephens' second, who would soon succeed him. Now, I did not know what to say to this man of the hour, who bore my son's given name. Powderly put out his hand and, with a firm grip, shook my own.

"Did you care for the speech?" His eyes glimmered at me.

"Grand, so," I managed to speak up at last.

"Ah, you're from Cork, I had cousins there."

"North Cork, by way of Memphis." I said.

"And what made you come here tonight?"

"My husband was a strong union man."

"I see." He noted the past tense. "Your name?"

"Mrs. George Jones," again my voice held pain and pride.

"Come back, Mrs. Jones, and feel free to speak out."

I did both and found that the floor didn't cave in.

"I have a question..." I began, the next night.

"Ask away, that's why I'm here," Powderly said.

I cannot recall why I challenged him that time, but he never let me forget that exchange. He says he remembers me as good-looking, with a quick mind and a quicker tongue — he could not resist adding that last. We soon became life-long friends, though we didn't always agree.

Terence called walk-outs and strikes "barbaric" tactics; I thought that they were a damn good idea. He was the idealist; I, the pragmatist. Still, as years passed and the labor movement grew quickly, he came to see that strikes could be useful to bring about change. Others were starting to use them and some even made progress. I got caught up in lively discussions in that old church and in that unofficial branch of the Knights. Meanwhile, after meetings, we managed to leave disagreements behind. Whenever Terence was there in Chicago, we'd meet his wife, Emma, down at "The Lep."

We'd talk about everything except labor. In time, I opened my heart to them about George and our children. To this day, the Powderlys remain my closest friends. I've smuggled letters out of this jail cell to them and they, in turn, have smuggled words of encouragement in here to me. Terence, now an attorney and Mayor of Scranton, has helped with my legal defense.

Since that first encounter with him, decades have passed and much has happened — in a blink, it now seems. I'll always think of Terence as a kind of midwife at the long birthing of Mother Jones.

■

« 11 »

S o...." The reporter stares into my jail cell.
"So?" I stare back, ever wary around the press.
"What were you doing in the seventies, eighties?"
"Learning." I keep it short and not too sweet.
"Learning how?" This reporter resembles a whippet.
"Going to meetings, rallies, the usual things."
"Nothing usual about you." His voice turns oily.
"What is it you're after?" My guard goes up.
There is a pause; I wait for his pounce.
"Any truth to the story that you ran a brothel?"
"You wish. Can't you boys give that one up?"
Another pause; again, I brace.
"What about your love affair with Terence Powderly?"
"What love affair?" I leap from my stool.
"Well, that touched a nerve." He makes a note.
"Lies and smears tend to affect me that way."
"Can't find much of your early years with labor."
"Who sent you here?" I snap. "The Devil himself?"
"Back to the seventies, eighties, what you recall."
"Back then...." Thinking, I find myself trailing off.

Finally, the reporter gives up and leaves.

Back then, there was so much happening in Chicago. The city was rebuilding so fast, people still talk about that with pride. The place was a magnet for folks seeking jobs — especially new immigrants who were willing to work at the lowest of wages. They filled the halls of the Knights of Labor all over the country, I heard. Then, when hard times hit us in '73, there was a financial panic and, of course, the working poor suffered the most. Employers cut wages; our meetings swelled. Employers cut jobs; our halls overflowed.

I began by passing out leaflets at meetings, filling cups with steaming coffee, and taking in everything I could. Uriah Stephens, still the Knights' leader, worked hard, assisted by my friend, Terence Powderly. I learned from them both during the seventies and the early eighties, when trade guilds were turning into America's first large unions. When I look back now, I see that I joined the labor movement just as it was coming of age. I guess we grew up together. Still I was startled when Terence approached me with a new idea:

"Mary, would you make a speech at a meeting?"

"Me? You're serious?" I was truly taken aback.

"You're educated, well-spoken," Uriah began.

"And you were a school teacher," Terence added.

"And you come from the working poor." Uriah said.

"I guess I'm some kind of a mongrel," I laughed.

"You're a rarity," Uriah said. "And yes, we're serious."

"Your husband was union," Terence said quietly.

I guess he knew that would clinch it for me.

The first time I gave a speech, I had to stand on an orange crate so the big audience could see me — just over five feet tall, in my usual black dress. I wondered if these tough men would laugh at this little woman before them. To my amazement, no one did. I lifted my voice as I'd done, years before, in the school room, and heard that voice carrying throughout the hall.

I don't recall what I said in that speech; afterwards, for the first and last time, I was dizzy. "You'll get over that fast," Terence predicted. He was right. I discovered that I could tell stories from my perch on the orange crate, and stories captured people's attention. I had plenty of struggles to speak of and I used them to hearten my listeners.

They needed to be heartened. The times were troubled and the early strikes brought turbulence with them. Although it failed, I learned from "The Great Uprising" of '77 — that first national railroad strike, lasting two weeks, and making way for others to follow. I was there on the scene, passing out leaflets, when Chicago laborers struck the McCormick Reaper Company for higher wages. Soon I learned that many workers, skilled and unskilled, worked sixteen hour days. I spoke out with Terence and others who pushed for an eight-hour work day — and I stood in the rain, watching in horror as Chicago's Haymarket Rally literally blew up in our faces.

All the way, through the failures and bloodshed and slow progress, I stayed with the Knights of Labor, though Haymarket was a great setback for us. By that time, I was well used to setbacks and I could speak from the heart about fighting on. Evenings, I went to labor meetings all over town. Mornings, I went off to my sewing clients. After I'd made some more money, I'd moved to a simple room in quieter boarding house. My business picked up, but I still walked to jobs with the tools of my trade wrapped up in my shawl. That was exactly the way I wanted it, though few understood this and I did not care to explain.

Never again did I have my own home or my own shop.

Never again did I want either one.

I could not bear the thought of losing them once again. As an itinerant seamstress, I had more freedom for union work. As a woman alone, I had more time for my own pursuits. And, I believed, if I was going to work with the poor, I should be one with them. The Powderlys asked me if I ever got lonely. I was too busy for that, I would say — a half-truth; I think they understood.

And I think they understood another certainty, though we did not discuss it. To my way of thinking, I was still married; there could never be another husband for me. By then, I'd come to realize that the pain of my losses would never leave me. I would carry it with me, then, like the tools I brought with me, wrapped up in my shawl. Deliberately, then, I chose the life of a wanderer, a lodger, a worker, and an apprentice union organizer. After all I'd survived, I feared no one now.

I felt a rightness about my decision. One night, at a labor meeting, I climbed onto the orange crate and looked out at the crowd. As my voice rose, I realized that I did not stand there alone. I stood with my grandfather Harris and his Whiteboys. I stood with my father, Richard Harris, and his Ribbonmen. I stood with the iron-molders of Local 66 and their fine women.

And I stood with and for my husband, George Jones.

~~

By the time Eugene Debs took on the Pullman empire, I was a full-fledged labor organizer, with my own publication: *Appeal To Reason.* As I handed it out on the street corners, I talked union to hundreds of people.

I always stood out because I was a woman, and oddly enough, my black dresses made me contrast with more colorful folk. I always wore my trademark hat with the pansies; my hair, now, was streaked with gray. I hated wearing spectacles, but I couldn't avoid the damn things any longer.

When I glanced in a mirror now, I thought I resembled a schoolmarm far more than I did when I was still teaching. I must have cut an unusual figure, which came in useful, and use it I did. People had started to recognize me by 1890, the year I turned fifty-three.

That year, the Knights of Labor merged with a sister union to create a new outfit entirely: The United Mine Workers. I'm proud to say that about 20,000 miners, joined up that first year. Still, out of 250,000 miners, that was not nearly enough.

For the UMW, I took a train to West Virginia to gain more new members. As far back as I can remember, I'd known the perils of mining; there were several mines in County Cork. I'd overheard stories of cave-ins and explosions; sometimes, I'd seen weary men with blackened faces, on their way home. These images came back to me in West Virginia, where I got a closer look at mining's brutalities.

It wasn't only the workers who lived with harsh conditions. I visited mining families in their tar-paper shacks — all owned by the mining company, along with the store, the school, and even the community's newspaper. I did not realize, then, how deeply these people would touch my soul. Nor did I realize that I was known to the mine operators. They'd heard of that successful strike in Arnot.

I figured that one out the minute I got off the train in a small town called Norton. Its miners had gone out on strike for higher wages and safer conditions. I knew this would likely be a loss for them, but it seemed wrong to favor the fights we could win. Still, I hadn't expected Norton to be quite that tough. Right there, at the depot, I received a blunt message from the mine superintendent: "Get out now — or get your brains blown out."

All right, I thought. Here we go.

"Sorry, Ma'am," the messenger added.

"You tell the superintendent this." I kept my gaze level.

The miner seemed to flinch but I went on.

"I'm not here to see him, I'm here to see the miners."

"All the same Ma'am...you need a guard...armed."

"I'll be all right," I said, but the miner shook his head.

"Who's that?" I saw a burly man following us.

"He's looking out for you." The miner sounded grim.

Of course, the company men barred me from holding meetings on "their" turf, but an A.M.E. Zion church, with black members, offered to let me speak in their sanctuary. I bless them to this day. Soon there were folks trickling in to the meeting, and then more, and then a large crowd. I did not dare stand in the pulpit, but I stood up front and started to speak.

"Brothers and sisters," I began.

"Ma'am." The minister laid a hand on my arm.

"I can guess," I said. "The company owns this building?"

He nodded. "We'll lose our church if we let you talk."

"I'm sorry, Reverend — move on."

"My apologies, Ma'am." He looked stricken.

"None needed, we'll meet out on the highway."

The crowd stayed with me as we moved to the nearest crossroads; there I stood on another crate and began to speak once again. And, once again, I was interrupted. I'd learned to be prepared for all kinds of interference. I saw the burly man edge toward me but this time, I got off easy. The man was a mine guard and, if he could, he would break up this meeting.

"How dare you?" He shouted at me.

"This is a public highway," I reminded him.

"You took an armed man into God's house."

"That wasn't God's house today," I snapped..

"Then what was it?" The guard called.

"That was the coal company's house."

"Is that right?" He blinked but stayed put.

"Didn't you know God Almighty doesn't onto company land?"

Over my spectacles, I stared him down.

The crowd roared and we had ourselves a fine meeting out there on the road. Afterwards, I visited mining families and slept on the floor in one of their shacks. Whenever I pillowed my head on my purse, I'd recall how I'd sat on that bag in Old Saint Mary's Church, after Chicago's great fire. Even that had been practice for my present work, I thought, as I held another crossroads union meeting. Even so, as I'd suspected, the Norton strike failed in the end. I told the miners that I would return. It took me years, but return I did.

Meanwhile, there were others who needed a visit from me — the odd little woman in black, so maternal in appearance — so fiery in speech. I didn't realize for a while that "Mother Jones" was slowly becoming my new name

~~.

Hip-boots and black skirts: that was my uniform for tramping West Virginia's gullies and hills.

That's how the miners there say they recall me: a "lady" with a flowered black hat, a simple black dress — and waders, beneath. I bless my physical constitution: it's held up a long time, much abused. As I'd told my husband, we "famine Irish" have always been strong. I would need that strength as I left Norton — with my brains intact — and went wherever I was sent.

I often thought of the map on my school rooms' walls. Now, years after drilling my students on states' names, I found myself learning them over again, in a way I'd never expected. I used to feel as if I'd stepped directly into that map of America.

"Class, what's the capital of Alabama?" I used to ask.

"Bir-ming-ham" my students would chorus back to me.

And now, I was right there, on union business.

I was there when that brave labor leader, Eugene Debs, challenged the Pullman Palace Car Company. Debs' parents were immigrants from Alsace and he'd worked the railroads since he was twelve. His challenge took the form of another strike that shut down hundreds of train tracks in several states. The issues were wages and safety and Eugene worked hard. Still, the strike failed and Debs went to jail for a while. In the short run, he'd lost; in the long run, railroad men would come to benefit, I believed.

Meanwhile, I went on with my work, though Birmingham was an armed city, under martial law. I was forbidden to hold meetings there, but I found a way — nor was it hard. I'd size up the lines of soldiers on guard, and quietly, always smiling, I would slip right through them. I must have looked like someone's grandmother, off to crochet lace doilies with more sweet old ladies. Once I got beyond the militia, I went to the mining camps — and went ahead with the meetings I'd planned.

I held many, in secret, under cover of night, and there I was in Alabama, when Debs was released from jail. With other organizers, I laid plans to give Debs a hero's welcome, and to show the miners' support for the rail strikers' cause. Birmingham's workers were thrilled to host such an occasion; they chose the Opera House for its locale. Then came the injunction from the mayor's office:

No meetings permitted — the Opera House must close its doors.

All right, I thought, once again:

Here we go.

I handed out leaflets and visited workers until I thought I'd raised a fair crowd. The word must have passed through the grapevine pretty fast; I wasn't expecting the thousands of miners who came together at Birmingham's depot. The train pulled in and Eugene

Debs got off, looking thinner now, his bald head shining. He pumped his fist then, and those miners did not wait for the gates to open — they jumped right over the railings. As I watched, the men hoisted Debs up onto their shoulders and carried him out of the station, trailed by the crowd, half singing, half chanting: *Debs, Debs, Debs.* I guess the militia had orders to stand back that time, or maybe our numbers just looked too daunting.

Without any violence or one single challenge, we marched through the city, right past the office of the mayor and the chief of police. As we neared the Opera House, its owner had a sudden change of mind. The hall's great doors swung open and we gathered there in peace. What a sight we must have been: on the red carpet, rough men in coveralls, slapping backs under the shimmering of grand chandeliers.

"The churches were empty that night," I wrote to Terence and Emma. "And that night the crowd heard a real sermon by a preacher whose message was one of human brotherhood."

■

« 12 »

Medieval West Virginia:

Its tent colonies on the bleak hills, its grim men and women. When I get to the other side, I shall tell God Almighty about West Virginia.

For many years, on and off, I worked through that state. Firsthand, I got to know its hills and ravines. I avoided hotels and rooming houses — instead I stayed with the miners' families, who shared with me what little they had. I was both organizer and friend to those folk, but unionizing there was tough duty, all the same.

Those coal miners were the lowest paid workers in America. Their work, of course, was dank, dark, and dangerous, down among rich seams of top dollar coal. I knew why the place was so hard to organize: the companies owned every part of those miners' lives. If someone got out of line, the company would punish him and his family, denying them entry to the company store, the company school — even the company doctor. Of course, the mining community was leery of joining the union. When the UMW put me in charge of southern

West Virginia, I knew we were in for a long battle. I was a bit over sixty then, still strong and healthy, but wondered if I would live to see any real change.

I set up my headquarters in Montgomery and sent reports to John Mitchell, the UMW president at that time. Always, I asked him to send me stronger organizers. Meanwhile, our meetings began to pull in more folks. We didn't wait for them to come to us — we went to them, treading steep paths in our sturdy boots. Sometimes, with my crew, I walked five miles or more to get to these meetings. Sometimes, on the way back, late at night, we'd walk up the train tracks to find our way. It was almost like sleepwalking; I'd count the railroad ties to stay awake.

I didn't realize how much this meant to the miners — the sight of me tramping through their terrain. I wasn't off in some city's boardroom; I was there with the people, out in the field. I came to know many of them, face-to-face. To my mind, there was no other way. It had to be personal, whatever that took.

"My children—" I broke off at the start of one speech.

Why had I said that?

I paused for moment, unable to steady my voice.

My own children would have been the same age as these folks.

You'll have other children, that old midwife had predicted.

Not these children, I had sobbed.

Different children, the midwife had promised.

Was this what she meant? Was this what she saw?

I had not thought of her words in years.

"My children," I began again. "Let me tell you about your lives."

There was a long expectant silence. I looked up and went on.

"Let us consider this together."

Folks gathered closer.

"I'm one of you. And I know what it is to suffer."

The crowd quieted and drew closer still.

I described a miner's life from start to finish: "Breaker boys" at work with the coal from the age of eight; the long dripping darkness that lay ahead; the bruised hands and black dust in lungs; the chance, every day, of sudden death in a cave-in or fall. And yet, this labor fueled the entire nation. A sigh of recognition rose from the crowd.

"I stayed with a miner's family where the father earned nothing at all for his work. Ten tons of coal went for rent, the doctor, the blacksmith, the water, powder and oil, with nothing left over," I told them; I watched them nod and shout out a single word: "*Yes*."

Then I made my voice low and intense to challenge each man.

"Why allow others, no more God's sons than you, take from you all the wealth you produce?" I let that question hang in the air for a long moment. No one spoke.

"You may pity yourselves," I told them, flat-out. "But you do not pity your brother, or you would stand together to help one another. Wake up, my boys — you can still have better lives. Join the union, boys, and fight as one. A new day awaits you — I know this from my own experience. I belong to a class that has been robbed, exploited, and plundered down many long centuries. Because I belong to that class, I have an instinct to help break our chains — and if I, a frail woman can do it, can't you?"

"We can," the miners called out.

"What's that?" I looked at them.

"*We can*," they shouted back.

"We can do it together, can't we?"

I saw tears on the faces before me.

"Mother Jones, yes, we can."

Stunned to hear the word, "Mother," I paused.

An old man pushed forward; I stepped aside.

"God, God, no one else talks to us that away."

I heard his voice in my sleep, that night and for many nights to come. Somehow, those folks' voices meant more to me than a reporter's voice in *The Washington Post*: "Her earnestness would carry conviction to a steel magnet itself. When she predicted hope of improvement for the great mass of American toilers, her face glowed...."

I kept that clipping, sent on by John Mitchell, to read when I had a setback or defeat. But that time, we won out there, near the Kenawah River. A small piece of West Virginia that I'll not need discuss with Almighty God. Until ten years later.

~~

In West Virginia, you couldn't step on a piece of ground without stepping on an injunction.

This was especially true in the northern part of the state, where John Mitchell sent me. He said the coal companies up there had scared our boys and some had been brutally beaten. Johnny said he didn't like to keep sending me out to take dangerous fields, but he knew I'd be willing. Of course, I was, even though I was second in command there, after another Irish-Catholic organizer, Tom Haggerty, from Pennsylvania. My first task was spiriting food in to the striking miners near Monongah: the site of the strike camp. Once again, I went out among the local farmers and their wives. Together, we organized "pound parties," where each farming family brought a pound of home-grown food.

Things were starting out fine; so I thought. I began to feel lucky — always and ever, for me, a bad sign. In short order, the Fairmont Coal Company stopped us with an injunction: no more meetings. It was done all legal and proper, through the courts. It was known that the companies had several judges in their pockets; this judge moved faster than most. Young Tom Haggerty was arrested and John Mitchell sent word that I was in charge. The task was daunting there; the coal companies were fewer but stronger, forming a kind of monopoly.

I held meetings and rallies, as usual. The prevailing wisdom was "agitate and educate," well before organizing a union. The usual plan of action began with speeches, leaflets, and planting seeds. In places, this could take a long time. I wanted to move things a bit faster. I repeated my practice of meeting with miners in secret, by night, to form a UMW local. Many times, if one of the boys couldn't spring for the fifteen dollar dues for a charter, I put up the money myself.

Even so, I didn't get nearly as far as I'd hoped. These mine operators went out and hired themselves some burly "guards." These were thugs, plain and simple and, like all thugs, they didn't hold back. Sometimes, men who joined the union were blacklisted — or shot dead. They were ambushed and beaten. Numbers of them just disappeared, leaving no trace behind. Storekeepers were threatened if they did any business with union families. It took a hell of a lot of courage for men to stick with us.

With those who stayed strong, we met at night in the woods, in stables and barns. Miners drew coded maps on large boulders to show the way to our secret gatherings. Sometimes, I had to ask other organizers to join me for a night hiding out on a river bank. Those thugs meant business; murderous business. We would hear bullets whiz past us as we sat huddled between boulders, our black clothes protecting us, as we blended in with the darkness.

Huddling there with those union men, I felt fiercely protective; they were, after all, in my charge. I couldn't let anything happen to them. When one bullet flew near, singing through the air over our heads, I pulled the boys down as low as I could. Young Tom Haggerty, out on bail, was with us. Crouching together, I could smell damp earth and night-dew and sweat. Peaceable scents — laced with gunpowder.

"Jesus," Tom said. "This isn't unionizing — this is *war*."

We ducked as another bullet whistled past.

"I didn't sign on for *this*," said Al, one of my newest organizers.

"If you'd grown up in Ireland," I whispered, "this would seem like business as usual."

"I grew up in Milwaukee," Al snapped. "This ain't usual there."

There was a silence. Above us, the sharp stars started to fade.

"No," I agreed. "This shouldn't be 'usual' anywhere atall."

"I mean, what the hell?" Al whispered back. "Why do this?"

Another silence. When I spoke, finally, my voice was quiet.

"I guess there is a line. There you stand up — or turn away."   "That's one tough line," Al said after a while.

After that night, we lost him to Milwaukee. With families at home, other organizers began to quit — but I held out as long as I could.

Near unionized Flemington, I stood up to speak in the Willow Tree Schoolhouse. About 300 brave folks had gathered there. The smells of the place were familiar to me: inkwells and wood, apples and books. Sunlight slanted over the desks where people perched. Behind me was a blackboard; for just a moment, I felt secure. I opened the meeting and managed to get halfway through my speech, when a federal marshal opened the door. He took one look at me and served me with a writ. This came from the United States District Court of Judge John L. Jackson, the marshal intoned. Jackson had slapped us with another injunction — this one shut down all strikers' speeches and rallies. I accepted the writ, kept my voice level, and finished my talk. After all, I told the marshal, the writ did not take effect until midnight. I could damn well talk till then.

The marshal was not pleased.

All right, I thought.

Here we go, once again.

I paced through the night, thinking of my father's Ribbonmen. Toward dawn, I decided to defy the injunction. I knew I'd likely land myself in jail but maybe, in the end, this would raise a protest and help the strikers. Our team of organizers passed out reams of handbills all over Clarksburg ahead of my speech, nearby. I remember that June was so clear, cool, and fine. Roses were blooming as we rode to the meeting where I would speak for about half an hour.

We had a good crowd, despite what we called the "thug factor," and I stepped to the podium. I adjusted the lace at my throat and began my talk. I was ten minutes into it when I saw marshals moving through the crowd, arresting our organizers. Then I sensed a presence just to my left. It was a tall, red-faced marshal who informed me that I was also under arrest.

"Wait till I finish," I snapped and the crowd started to laugh. The marshal looked confused. At that point, I had nothing to lose. I went ahead and bluntly stated what everyone knew: the mine operators had pressured the judge and the press. I guess that was just a bit too much for the marshal assigned to me. His heavy hand fell like a hoof on my arm.

"Goodbye, boys," I called out. "I'm under arrest. I may go to jail." The marshal tugged at my sleeve, but I wasn't done. "I may not see you for a long time. Pay no attention to the injunction machine in Parkersburg..." The marshal had enough and pulled me away. I lost my temper and offered one last shot: "While you serve humanity, that judge serves injunctions; while you starve, he plays golf—" Without ceremony, I was jerked away.

The Wood County jail in Parkersburg, West Virginia, is not a bad place — better than some rooming houses I've known. No rats, no roaches, no wretched conditions. The jailor and his wife kept the place spanking clean and were kind to me. Meanwhile, the union would appeal our charges — contempt, that was certain — and if the appeal failed, he would take our case to the President of the United States. Brave words. The truth was this: we were losing the northern half of West Virginia. Injunctions were shutting our movement down.

At our trial, the red-faced judge glared at me. So much for "blind justice." Still looking at me, he called us "busybodies" who created dissatisfaction. Then, he ruled that my last meeting went against both his order and the protections of free speech. He expressed shock that I, a woman of "apparent" intelligence would let myself be used by agitators as a "tool." He shook his head and his finger at me and advised me that I should do as the "Allwise Being" intended for my sex: to pursue charity work, the "true sphere of womanhood."

I know, I know — I lost my temper again. It wasn't prudent to call Judge Jackson "a scab." Later in Chambers, I told Judge Jackson that I had seen my duty, had done it, and would do it again. The Judge pressed his fingers together and studied me. I figured I was going to spend a long time in that nice county jail, but the judge let me off, saying he would not let me don the martyr's cloak and "force my way into jail." Six of the organizers did time. Unionization had come to a halt in West Virginia for a long while. Ten years, in fact. And I was on the scene once again. Before then, I had other places to go.

■

« 13 »

Memphis: our old neighborhood, "Pinch," opens before me.

Easily, I find my way to our old home on Winchester Street. The house looks just the same and the door is unlocked. I push it gently and it swings open, silently drawing me back inside. Without a sound, I cross the familiar threshold and enter the main room downstairs. Of course, it is empty, but sun-streaked and bright.

Out in the kitchen, and I note that the cast-iron stove is still there. It looks oddly beautiful, this everyday piece. I turn toward the stairs and, as I climb them, I recall passing this way with freshly washed sheets, piled in my arms. I turn toward our room — our bedstead stands there, after all this time. How solid it seems — how welcoming. Late at night, George would wait there, watching as I let down my hair.

The house seems to hold its breath as I move on now toward the children's room. Their beds remain, with the trundle and cradle. Sunlight shines from the wood I so carefully polished. The house is held in that sweet afternoon lull, while my husband would work and my children would play. At this time of day, I'd brew a pot of strong tea and sit in the kitchen, planning our supper, thinking of leeks and potatoes and luck. Let my mending basket overflow, let the laundry pile high — even so, I knew that I was the luckiest woman in this great green world.

The dream lingers, then suddenly breaks.

I wake with a jolt in the Walsenburg jail.

In my mind, I've returned to "Pinch" many times, though I've never gone back in reality — I never will. But that dream has followed me though the years and for a long while, it would leave me in tears. After I had left Memphis, I noticed how my hands would shake around children. I used to wonder: Would these quiet tremors ever let up? Frankly, I doubted it; grief such as mine wasn't likely to heal. But after I went down to Birmingham, something began to change deep within me.

In Alabama, I started a pilgrimage through a long chain of textile mills. In these factories, I was asked to take a series of jobs, "undercover." My mission: to see if conditions were ripe for unionizing. I traveled, I worked, I observed carefully — and somewhere along the way, my hands stopped shaking. The sight of those pallid mill children affected me so, I guess my grief turned into rage. After my West Virginia stint, I felt drawn back into that old fury — begun years before in pockets of hell.

~~

In Birmingham I'd heard mill stories before my excursion. I made sure that I learned the basic facts: The textile business hired more children than any other industry. Most of these children were girls, just a few years older than my two oldest daughters had been.

Despite some weak laws, there were four-year-old children helping out in the mills — for no pay. Wages for a thirteen-year-old might come to a couple of dollars a week and that week was six days long; each day's work lasted ten hours. I could tell that these figures were already roiling my blood.

I read other reports on the work children did. Because they were small, they had dangerous tasks: they were ordered to slip under huge machines, oil them, and then replace the spindles— night shifts and day shifts alike. I was startled to learn that almost two million children worked in mills, up North as well as the South. And perhaps because they were so helpless, they had no voice; no advocate, few laws to protect them.

These facts piqued my curiosity but still, they meant little until I could put faces with them. And then, in Cottondale, Alabama, statistics turned shockingly personal.

I remember strolling up to that first mill — the sunlight was blinding. For this occasion, I'd stowed my black clothes and put on a calico dress; nothing fancy but pretty enough. My hair was still red then and I topped it off with a straw hat. I wanted to look like a good prospect for employment, but I was nearly thrown by the mill superintendent's first question:

"Any children?" A sallow-faced man studied me.

"Why, sir?" Off guard, I caught my breath.

"We hire families — more hands to work."

"I see, yes, of course." I tried to recover.

"How big's your family, Ma'am?"

I paused again, then spoke carefully.

"Our family, there were six of us."

"Ah, they're on their way here?"

"Never far." I tried to look him in the eye.

"Good news," he said. "You got yourself a job."

I was given a broken-down company shack with torn oiled paper in the windows. The door wouldn't close and the walls had wide cracks. I did not complain, only took note and tried to get the place cleaned up. This, then, was what the mill company's housing was like — worse than I'd expected. And I was still reeling from my interchange with the super about my family. It amazed me how suddenly, with a word or a glance, the pain could bite deep.

That day, I kept myself busy with mop, broom and scrub brush, interspersed with several trips to the pump. At dusk, I felt the stares of the workers, trudging trudged home. Their faces were weary; my presence was a passing novelty.

For a short while, oil lamps lit the surrounding windows and the smell of fried sausages rose on the air. While I ate a sandwich, I listened to the sleepy voices of children. To my surprise, I saw few of them outside; they were mostly too tired to play, I soon discovered. A woman's voice drifted toward me as she sang a child to sleep: *Hush, little baby, don't say a word, Papa's gonna buy you a mockingbird...*

With all my resolve, I found myself forcing back tears. Around eight-thirty, by my pocket watch, the whole place quieted down and slowly went dark. I sat in my window and watched how the shacks leaned together, as if for comfort, under a full moon. This was company land, company housing, and down the road was the company store. If it could, I figured, the company would own the very moonlight that fell across this poor village, giving its many torn windows a shine.

~~

The next morning, at four-thirty sharp, the mill whistle shrieked like an overwrought demon. There was a sudden stirring in the shacks all around me. After I'd come to know the families there, I learned what was happening behind the walls. On rough wooden floors, straw beds were swiftly emptied. Children as young as six crouched at rickety tables, while their slack-faced mothers fed them cornbread and coffee; cottonseed oil took butter's place. Flimsy clothes were pulled on. There were no shoes to tie. Hair was hastily combed and tied back. And then, in a massive procession, the whole army of serfs trotted off, myself among them, to start work at five-thirty; not one moment later. The sky was still dark when we left the shacks and when we returned at day's end, darkness was closing in.

In between, there was no sunshine for us, only the mill's dim light. And there was powerful presence lying in wait: a great tide of noise. This hit us in the face like a wave; as I entered the mill I stood stunned for a moment. Never had I known such a din, crashing over us throughout the day. Machinery clattered, banged, and whirred without ceasing. I realized why so many mill workers started to lose their hearing early on — for an hour a day, then for longer spells; then forever. I thought I might go deaf, myself, that first day. To me, this constant clamor seemed like iron rain. Lint snowed through the stagnant air. People coughed and wheezed, but the foremen made sure they kept up the pace.

There was a brief break at noon for more coffee and cornbread; then the shift went on. The children caught my eye as I stood at my station. They looked wan and listless, yet their hands still moved. Quickly, I understood why I didn't see them running about outside; they were simply too worn out. Sleep was their recreation, their release, as play is to a free child. Those who were sixteen and younger earned ten cents a day.

Toward the end of a shift, some of the children's heads began to nod over their work. I had to hold myself back when I saw the mill's manager wake them with cold water, thrown in their faces. This was hard enough for anyone's sight, but to a mother's eyes, it was unbearable. I looked away, clenching my fists and my jaw. Looking back now, I think that these mills were more wrenching to me than the coal mines, where men could fight back.

One week in Cottondale was more than enough for me. I noticed the super kept watching my movements — and kept demanding when my children would come. Dodging the question, I packed up my few things and moved on to Tuscaloosa. There I worked in that rope factory, where I came to know that great strength of twine — like the strength that seems to flow through my kin. I learned other things in Tuscaloosa, though, and these had more to do with weakness.

I remember a scrawny man, maybe thirty-six, who was so worn by toil, I thought he was twice his age. Since he was a boy, he had worked in the mill, and for the last few years, he made forty cents a day at an old loom. His daughters, six and seven, were so thin, their limbs looked like sticks. Between them, these small girls presided over some 155 spindles.

Again, the mother in me ached at the sight of them and their co-workers. Folks there were so poor, children were encouraged to work — not only by the mills but by their own parents. I saw that this was a complicated situation, but still, I knew, a union would help raise wages.

I governed my tongue, though, especially at dawn, when the children lurched off the long night shift. The mill was kept overly warm and the children would shiver as the cold air hit them. Not one had a coat or even a shawl; most wore thin, patched clothes. Passing them was another grim procession going toward the mill. I'll always remember that long gray line of children with their dinner pails, coming in for the day shift.

~~

I was reaching the point where I had to do something — but I had no clear plan in mind. And so I kept moving throughout the South. Each new town, each new mill, brought me a new shock.

One of the worst was a place in South Carolina where pregnant women were "advised" to give birth in the factory itself. The new mother would rest for a few hours, then return to her loom, with her infant beside her in a blanket-lined box. I remembered my own hard labor with our first child and knew how exhausted and sore those women must be. Each evening, in my shack, I thanked God that my children's lives, though brutally short, had not been the lives of these mill babies, cradled in cardboard and later let loose to crawl through on the filthy floor, through forests of spindles.

I guess I was ready to act by the time I met Delia, my next-door neighbor a Kentucky mill town. She was tall and rawboned, with big eyes and long tawny hair; this she put up for work and warned me to do the same. Long hair could get caught in those textile machines; it had happened before.

I knew this story all too well, before Delia told me about a girl named Maggie. This story had traveled through the grapevine and I knew it was true; I was there to watch it unfold. In Selma, Alabama, I had taken a temporary job at yet another mill. I still remember Maggie and her mother, Nora; they had taken me in and I shared their shack for a while.

Maggie could not have been more than eleven years old, but she was already worn out from mill work. Her skin was fair and pale; even her freckles had faded. Still, she was a pretty girl and her mother predicted that Maggie would grow up to be a beauty. Even so, Maggie had no airs about her. She was welcoming to me and I couldn't help thinking of my daughter, Lizzie, whenever I saw this lovely young girl.

One Sunday, I recalled, some young friends came by Nora's shack. They wanted Maggie to come out with them for a picnic but she could not get out of bed. Her hair, long and coppery-red like mine, was fanned out over her flimsy pillow. Her green eyes flickered open when Nora tried to wake her — and I'll never forget what she said: "Oh Mother, just let me sleep; that's a lot more fun. I'm so tired I just want to sleep forever."

At the time, Nora and I sighed, but felt no sense of foreboding. The next day, a Monday, Nora and Maggie went off to start their week at the mill. That evening, I was there when two men appeared with Maggie in their arms. They laid her out, dead, on the kitchen table. Her hair had caught in the machinery and torn off her scalp.

There was a terrible silence after Delia and I shared this story.

I shuddered; she sighed. But she only told me such stories after we'd come to know one another. That didn't take long, though she never discovered what my real job was.

"Hey," was the first word Delia spoke to me.

"Hey," I called back, trying to fit in.

"Where's your man?" She asked then.

"I'm a...widow." My voice still cracked on that word.

"Me, too," said Delia — and our bond was forged.

One evening, I heard her weeping. I wanted to go to her, but I feared I'd intrude. The next night, I heard the weeping again. When I heard this for three nights in a row, I knew that I couldn't ignore it again. At the risk of overstepping the bounds of our friendship, I knocked on the door of her shack. Delia had the kind of sudden smile that could light up a bat's nest. She gave me one of those, with a cup of black coffee and a seat on a stool. We sat at her wobbly table and talked of the weather, the mill; the usual chat.

I watched the lamplight streak over the table and touch a blurred photograph on the wall. It was a picture of the mill's men and I guessed that her husband's face was among them. At least, I thought wistfully, she still had her children: three small daughters, asleep on a single straw mattress. There, in that shabby gray room, they huddled together under the only bright spot: a hand-pieced patchwork quilt. In a low voice, I asked Delia if I could help her.

"I'm so ashamed." She let her hair curtain her face.

"You can tell me," I said. "I've had hard times myself."

"I can't tell you how much we owe the company."

"I'd understand — believe me, I've been broke."

There was a long silence; then Delia looked up.

"My husband left me in debt." She hesitated.

"It happens," I said. "He died suddenly, you said."

Another silence, longer than the one before.

"We owe...*thirty-six dollars*." A huge sum to her.

"Little by little, you can pay that off, can't you?"

"Never ever," she said, rubbing her dark-rimmed eyes.

"It'll be hard, I understand, but surely—"

"No, Mary." She touched my arm and explained.

Even though she and her daughters all worked long hours, they kept on falling behind. Each week, Delia paid the company rent. Each month, she paid for food from the company store. In addition, each month, she had to pay interest on the loan that covered the debt. The year before, after expenses, the family had saved only one dollar. "There's no way out for us," Delia said. "Never, no way."

Watching her, I thought of the times I'd felt trapped. I'd always remember how I'd sat alone through nights of grief in the Winchester House. I'd always remember how I stood through another night in Lake Michigan, knowing that I'd lost everything.

But I also recalled the people who finally reached out to me when I was most in need: the midwife, the union, the man on the ladder. Still, I had to consider what the union men might do if they caught me interfering in this situation. I considered what the mill boss might do as well. And then I took Delia's hand.

"I think I can help," I said. "Trust me?"

She nodded. "Just say what to do."

The next morning I quit my mill job and used the day to make certain arrangements. I found a farmer out in the country who'd done some work for the Underground Railroad. Without many questions, he agreed to let me borrow his wagon for a few hours after dark. I asked if he might throw in some burlap socks. Slowly, he nodded. When I left him, his white head was bent as he greased his axles; I'd told him we'd need a quiet ride. Next, I contacted some railroad boys I'd come to know in the course of the "Debs strike." They remembered me and promised me that their run tonight would include a stop at the mill town's depot.

As I waited through that long afternoon, I swept the floor of my shack and changed into my usual black dress, once again. The mill's superintendent had only seen me in calico, worn with a straw hat. He might not recognize me in these clothes; in any event, they would blend with the darkness.

At dusk, I picked up the farmer's wagon and drove it behind a stand of tall elm trees. There I waited for Delia and her daughters, as we had planned. Dusk turned into evening and nobody came. I fretted that Delia might miss the train; I wondered if she'd lost her nerve, after all. Finally, I spotted four human forms emerging from the darkness. One of the girls carried the photograph from the wall of their shack. Delia, herself, held the tightly folded family quilt. I put the four of them in the wagon's flat bed and covered them over with burlap sacking.

Slowly, we veered onto the dim road. It couldn't have taken us much time to reach the depot; even so, that ride seemed to stretch out for hours. I flinched at every tree's rustle, every owl's call, every shadow. From the back of the wagon, I heard faint whimpering. We reached the depot just as the train's light appeared down the tracks. Delia's family climbed down and stared at the oncoming locomotive. One of the girls cried out in fright. Of course — they had never seen a train before. As the engine screeched to a stop, I pressed a ten dollar bill into Delia's palm.

"God bless," she whispered. "Whoever you are."

"God bless," I whispered back. "Now go on — *Go.*"

I watched Delia's family climb onto the train and I waited until I could see them through the windows of the passenger car. I glanced behind me. No one was there. I glanced right and left — all was empty and calm. I lifted my hand to Delia; four streaming faces gazed out at me. They wept with relief, I knew, not regret. They were still waving as the train picked up speed and disappeared into the night.

Quickly, I returned the farmer's wagon and, before dawn, I had caught another train heading north. I never found out how the mill boss took the sudden absence of Delia's family. I watched the papers — there was no news of any pursuit. Certainly, the superintendent never knew who I was and could not connect me with Delia. I hoped that she could make a new start and stay out of the mills.

I often thought of her and her children — and all the mill children, seen and unseen. After that Southern excursion, I felt called to a fight against child labor. It would be a long struggle, I knew, and I would return to it many times throughout the coming years.

Once, as I spoke of this effort, I quoted the Gospel of Mark: "Suffer the little children to come unto me...for such is the kingdom of God." I remember that I looked up at the audience and added: "If Heaven is full of undersized, round-shouldered, hollow-eyed, listless sleepy angel children — Then I want to go to the other place with the bad little boys and girls."

■

« 14 »

Hello in there." The boy's voice sounds muffled.
I look up at the high window in my basement cell.
"Hello to you." I call to the boy who grins down at me.
"You're the 'March Lady,'" the boy shouts louder.
"I was...." I smile back, grasping what he means.
"My cousins back East, they marched with you."
"Grand, so. You saw pictures in the paper?"
"They kept all the clippings—"
Before he can finish, a soldier shoves him away.
Here at the Walsenburg jail, children often draw near,
scrooch down, and wave at me through that barred
window; it's just above street level. Everyday, through
that window, I watch people's feet: miners' feet in old
shoes; soldier's feet, well shod in government leather; the
shoes of women with the heels run down; the dilapidated
shoes of children; barefooted boys.
Most of those boys are too young to remember the
"March of the Mill Children:" so it has always been
called, ever since. A big undertaking, it was, designed to
boost the faltering fight against child labor. That was

over a decade ago. That year, at sixty-six, I had my first automobile ride. That year, Theodore Roosevelt was in the White House. That year, Philadelphia's Liberty Bell toured the nation. And that year, some eighty thousand children labored in textile mills.

I felt called to return to their cause once again. This time, I would not simply observe and make notes. This, I believed, was a moment for action. Inspired by the Liberty Bell's successful tour, I envisioned a demonstration that would travel as well — a children's march. This moveable protest could make a great impact, but it would be tough going. I still wonder how I got up the gumption to put it on. I guess, once more, it all came down to the children; as always, they roused the fierce mother in me. From the start, I understood, the end of the march was a long shot. This time, we'd aim high. Very high. I wanted to take this cause all the way to the President of the United States.

"We Don't Only Fight the Fights We Can Win."

Often, I tell this to new organizers — and often, those words don't go over too well. The young field workers want to "stamp out injustice" and win right away. I hate to dampen their dedication and zeal; they need both, in large measure. But over the years, I've learned that our efforts seldom end in quick victories. In this line of work, little gets tied up, neat and clean. You see some progress here, reversals there, or you see nothing at all, for some time to come. Maybe that's the hardest part of my work: taking on causes that yield few results — unless you can wait. So it was with the mill children's march, that steamy July of 1903.

~~

"Daring," the march was called.

"Outrageous," it was called.

"A drama," it was called that, too.

Of course it was — all that and more.

It damn well had to be.

This cause was already half-lost.

Early in 1903, I was called into a textile mill in Kensington, Pennsylvania. There, the workers had walked off their jobs in attempt to win better working conditions. When I got off the train in that dreary station, a hundred others flashed through my mind. I'd been through so many, they blurred together into one: signboards, benches, porters, spittoons. Often, though, when I stepped onto a new platform to face a new challenge, I would feel some sense of excitement.

Here, in Kensington, I felt something else: a sense of defeat came to me before I even reached the gray little town. I watched a boy push a wide broom across the floor of the platform. He looked listless and round-shouldered — as did the strikers, when I finally reached them. I tried to rally the strikers but there wasn't much support in town for them or their situation. There was even less for the issue of child labor.

"Why?" I asked a reporter. "Why not write about this?"

"Better talk to my publisher." He backed away.

"Why?" I asked several publishers, then.

"The mills own stock in our papers," they admitted.

"Well, I've got stock in these children," I told them.

"What does that mean?" One man looked uneasy.

"You'll see." I turned on my heel and left his office.

By that time, I knew how to pass out leaflets, slap notices up on lamp posts, and get out a crowd. Over my spectacles, I looked with pride at the large group of working parents and children who rallied in Philadelphia that June. I'd selected a special location: Independence Square. From there, we marched one mile to the lawn of the courthouse. We had a fine July day on our side — there was a cool breeze, I remember; the sky arched over us and Philadelphia's brick buildings seemed to glow in the sun. City officials had opened their windows and stared out, glancing from me to the crowd. They knew who I was and, as I had hoped, they heard part of the speech I gave on that lawn.

"Philadelphia's mansions were built on the broken bones, quivering hearts, and drooping heads of these children," I began.

As I talked on, I held up a mill child's right arm, so that all could see his maimed hand. I heard a murmur flow through the crowd. Then I picked up a skinny child in my arms. I wanted to show how light he was, just skin and bones — even a small woman like me could lift him. Then I glared through my spectacles at the officials, still gazing from their open windows.

"No child will be sacrificed on your altar of profit," I shouted to them. Swiftly, the men slammed down their windows. I watched several reporters move through the crowd. I recognized a man from *The New York Times*; I noted the presence of other New York papers, as well as the local press. I had learned to "count the house" like a theater producer and this gathering was a pleasure to count. If only I could keep up this momentum before the heat got us down. I was going to keep our destination as a surprise but, at that moment, I decided to name it.

"This is only the start of our march," I announced. "We are going all the way to Sagamore Hill, outside New York City, where President Roosevelt stays for the summer. " I watched the reporters scribbling in haste. "We are taking our case to this country's chief executive—"

There was a burst of hearty applause.

"We will demand a federal law to stop child labor."

I heard cheers as the newsmen wrote furiously.

"If we fail," I said, "it will not be for our lack of effort."

More cheers, more whistles, more stomping feet.

"Even if the President does not receive us—"

Hisses and booing rose from the crowd.

"— we still win, by touching the nation's heart."

I devoutly hoped so; I kept my doubts to myself..

Before we set out, I asked parents for their permission to let their children march. I wasn't surprised that many refused. We were embarking on a long journey — besides, many parents did not want to give up their children's small salaries. I tried to help them imagine a different picture from the one they knew: Their children going off to school in the mornings, rather than off to work in the mills. Some smiled and said nothing; some, less polite, told me to leave them and their children alone. But most agreed and gave consent. At first, many parents joined in the march, along with local strikers. There were so many plans to be made, I found myself staying up half the night.

I waited for Independence Day celebrations to stir everyone's spirits. On the evening of July Fourth, at a public picnic, I spotted a trio of children in costume; they performed for the crowd as a small fife-and-drum corps. *Perfect*, I thought. As fireworks bloomed in the skies overhead, I spoke to their parents. Flattered and thrilled, they quickly agreed to let this trio launch our group.

Three days later, the March of the Mill Children took its first steps: three hundred strong, we were, marching as one — not to mention four wagons filled with things we would need. The press followed us and sent daily dispatches in to their papers. Soon, we were the "human interest story" of the summer. The headlines referred to us as "Mother Jones's Army." This army's spirits were high as well, though I was a bit startled when the fife-and-drum trio kept playing "Marching Through Georgia." I took a seat in one of the wagons so I could watch the "army's" progress. I saw people come to the doors of their houses to watch us go by and soon, our route was lined with spectators.

Ahead of me, I saw determined marchers and a forest
of signs held up on sticks. *"We Want to Go to School,"* one
sign read, borne aloft by a small girl. *"We Want Time to
Play,"* read a young boy's sign. *"We Ask Only Justice,"*
read the sign that his tall father carried. Those first few
days made me proud — and, to my surprise, a bit sad. As
usual, the sight of children made me think of my own. I
shook my head and climbed down from the wagon to walk
side-by-side with the marchers up front.

~~

A hot red dawn.

The Farmers Almanac predicted temperatures in the
nineties.

By July tenth, when we neared Trenton, New Jersey,
we were down to a hundred marchers. I had expected
some dropping out, but not quite this soon. I still wonder
how it would have gone if the heat hadn't grown so fierce.
I worried about the children who had holes in their shoes
and I fretted, as any mother would, about the marchers
tramping on the dusty roads.

Still, I noticed, the remaining group seemed to be
having a hell of a good time. When we passed a brook or
a pond, I urged the children into the water to cool off. For
the first time, I wished I knew how to swim. The back of
my dress was wet and my corset was a silent torture. I
watched the young boys as they larked about in a stream,
splashing and dog-paddling and crowing, while I paced
the bank, terrified that someone might drown. Thank
God, no one did.

I made sure that each child had a knapsack and other
equipment: a tin cups and plates, knives and forks. From
the wagon, the older boys helped me lift down a cauldron
where I cooked supper over an open fire, out in a field. All
of this was a grand adventure for these children who had
been cooped up, all their lives. I couldn't help the mist in
my eyes as I saw boys bounding like colts through field,

stretching their arms out, as if to embrace this sudden freedom.

People came to stare at us over the fence, then drew closer. Quickly, I signaled the fife-and-drum corps to play — and I was sure to pass a hat through the growing crowd: a mellow, kindly crowd which filled the hat up to its rim. Then, one evening, there was a sudden rumble of wagon wheels on road near us. Two farmers pulled up with loads of fresh fruit, homemade. pies, and donated clothing. All of us went to the wagons to shake the farmers' hands — such kindness was almost as shock for these children.

We had gone forty miles by the time we tried to enter the city of Trenton. The police barred our way, though they had no injunction. The town didn't want any "outside agitators" and the mill owners didn't want us there at all. In my best grandmotherly voice, I wondered aloud if the police might like to take their noon meal with us?

A donated vat of chicken stew went into my cooking pot and, holding out their plates, the children drew near. Something about that sight moved the policemen who began to talk about their own sons and daughters. I didn't have to ask again for admittance to Trenton. After that lunch, the police stood aside — and we just ambled on into town.

In front of City Hall, a damn good crowd waited for us to arrive. About five thousand people were there, that hot day, as the light faded and a light breeze stirred the children's hair.

I stood up to address the gathering: "You are told that every American-born male citizen has a chance of being President. I tell you that the hungry man without a bed in the park would sell his chance for a good square meal, and these little toilers, deformed, dwarfed in body, soul and morality — they don't even have the dream that they might some day have a chance at the President's chair."

As I spoke, I spotted some newcomers: a group of women threaded their way through the crowd until they reached me. As soon as I stopped speaking, the women introduced themselves — these were the wives of the policemen we'd entertained at lunch.

The women whispered an offer to me. As I looked into their faces, I thought of the union women who had come to me, at the house on Winchester Street. I had a deep sense of trust about these women standing before me, still in their aprons. I agreed to their offer. I still catch my breath when I think of what happened: In their own homes, the policemen's wives put the children up for the night, gave them breakfast, and even gave them box-lunches for the next day's march. The children looked almost stunned by this kindness, so new to them — like a romp in the fields or a swim in a brook.

Even so, as we pressed on, more marchers grew tired and fell away. Worse, a grown man, a father of three, grumbled that I stayed in hotels while the rest of them sweated out the hot nights in the fields. It took all my strength to govern my tongue when I heard about this. Some nights, I went ahead of the marchers, to scout out new destinations; when I did that, I didn't want to camp out alone. I bitterly resented that man's criticism and for a short while I let it burn in my mind. Not for long, though — there were too many other pressing concerns. I was now worried about keeping the marchers on their feet — and getting to the President's home.

In Princeton, New Jersey, I watched the skies lower and darken. I had planned on camping, with permission, on the broad lawns of an estate. It belonged to former President Grover Cleveland who had answered my letter to him. I will always be grateful for his offer to let us stay there while the Cleveland family vacationed elsewhere.

But when I saw lightning split the sky, I knew I had to get the marchers in from those wide open lawns. I banged on the doors and the estate's caretaker came running out to us. Quickly, I tried to explain: We were expected; I showed him the letter.

The caretaker ran a hand through his gray hair and studied us with keen black eyes. There was a rumble of thunder; a new flash of lightening. The caretaker glanced from us to the sky and, without a word, led us into the sizeable barn, empty of horses. In short order, we piled bedrolls down from the wagon and that barn turned into a campsite for the night.

Some of the younger children were frightened by the storm. They drew nearer to me with each crash of thunder, until they were clinging to my skirts. I tried not to think of similar scenes in our "Pinch" house, where storms always sent our daughters running to our bed. There in that barn, once again, I heard children's voices call me, "Mother." Throughout the night, that word echoed in my head.

The next morning, with the mayor's permission, I gave a speech across from the grounds of Princeton University. I knew there were students and professors in the crowd assembled before me. Before the speech, I'd talked with a marcher; a ten-year-old boy named Jim Ashcroft. He had agreed to let me introduce him and talk about him — and I decided to speak with the same fire I used with the miners. These people, after all, were here to further their education.

"Look at this child," I pointed to Jim. "Here's a textbook in economics."

The crowd buzzed and waited for more; I gave it to them.

"See how stooped over he is? That's from carrying bundles of yarn weighting seventy-five pounds."

I paused, letting that fact sink in, and then I cut loose.

"He gets three dollars a week and his sister, who is fourteen, gets six dollars. They work in a carpet factory, ten hours a day, while the children of the rich are getting their higher education." I looked out at the crowd; it had gone silent now. "There are children all over the country who can't read or write because they work long shifts in the mills. Their bosses use the hands and feet of little children so they might buy automobiles for their wives and German Shepherds for their daughters to teach French. Study this situation for a while and you'll learn more than you ever expected."

Frankly, I waited for people to shrug this off, argue, or just walk away. This wasn't a crowd that threw rotten tomatoes, though I was prepared to field those. Still, they stayed through my talk and asked sharp questions. They got sharp answers. I truly enjoyed this exchange; it recalled those days when I'd challenge Terence Powderly at early meetings of the Knights of Labor. Later, expecting to be blistered in the press, I braced as an adult marcher brought me a newspaper.

"I guess I got scolded," I commented briskly.

"Not hardly." The sunburned man grinned.

"Not that I care," I added quickly; too quickly.

"It says you make other speakers sound like tin cans."

"Really?" I read the surprising words for myself.

"Thought you didn't care, huh, Mother?"

"Thought I didn't," I told him and pressed his hand.

~~

July Fifteenth. Another red dawn.

More amber fields rippling with heat.

The sky was white; the sun blazed like a forge.

When we camped on the banks of the Delaware River, a cloud of mosquitoes plagued us. Naturally, I feared these pests most of all. It was evident, though, that the bugs carried no disease; still, they got the marchers down, along with the weather. Every day, someone else dropped away. I could tell when someone was about to leave: first they would start avoiding my eyes. Then came the sheepish looks and sleeping positions near the edge of the group. The next morning, another marcher was gone.

I began to fear the whole thing would unravel too fast to leave an impact. Before we reached New York City, I sat down and composed a letter to President Roosevelt. It was hardly inflammatory. I merely described the lives of the mill children and asked him, as a father himself, to meet with us. There was no reply — I'd not expected one. This time.

Downtown in New York City, I held a meeting that drew thirty thousand people, going by police estimates. The tall buildings spiked all around me. Horns honked, traffic roared. I spoke louder. Then, fairly close, I saw four burly men in dark suits. They were staring intently at me. I continued my speech.

"We are quietly marching towards the President's home," I said.

"What do you hope to accomplish?" someone yelled out.

"I believe he can do something for these children."

The crowd applauded and shouted its approval. As the crowd broke up and we moved on, those men in dark suits stayed on our tail.

"Who are those thugs?" Jim Ashcroft asked me.

"Wish I knew." I was thoroughly baffled.

"I'll find out." Jim had a way with him.

"Take care," I called after the boy.

"You sound like my mother," he called back.

"I know I do," I admitted. "Sure, sue me, then."

With his huge dark eyes, long thin face, and floppy brown hair, Jimmy could appeal to anyone — and he knew how to use sweet-talk when it served him as well. He was stolid and faithful to me to the end of the march.

Meanwhile, he discovered that those men were Secret Service agents, assigned to protect the President against our tattered army — and against me. It didn't help matters, just then, when some reporter called me, "The greatest labor agitator of our age." A few days later, another headline appeared, calling me "Labor's Joan of Arc." I threw that paper away and did not keep the clipping. I knew too well what had happened to Joan of Arc. Probably, her captors were burly men in stiff dark clothes.

Morale was so low, I had to do something to raise the children's spirits. When we were offered a chance to visit Coney Island, I accepted within the hour. The marchers richly deserved a break — and where better than this great amusement park? It dazzled the children with its Ferris wheels and fancy rides. The whole place must have seemed like a fantasy land to them all: blinking lights, carny barkers, the smell of peanuts and cotton candy.

In the afternoon, I took the group to the beach and paced on the sand while they jumped through the waves. I counted their heads over and over and did not quit till everyone had come back on dry land. For the first time in my life, I wished I had learned how to swim. The back of my black dress was soaked and my stays were a silent torture. I hoped my hat would shield my face, but when I gave a speech that night, I know my fair skin was as red as the sunrise.

Meanwhile, I looked about for some way to use this singular setting. The man who ran the wild animal show agreed to let me speak to the crowd after his act was over. I had a notion I wanted to try. We needed more press; we needed some drama. After the lions and tigers had finished their act for the evening, their owner, Frank Bostwick, told his audience to stay on. Then he led the animals away to their keepers, leaving their cages empty. The place reeked of fur and sawdust; this made me sneeze, but other than that, and the wicked sunburn, all was going according to plan.

Quietly, I led Jim Ashcroft and his pals into the cages. The crowd let out a gasp. The children took up their positions, gripping the bars and gazing out at the audience. I watched as photographers jumped into action, along with a flurry of several reporters. Throughout my speech, the children held firm. I gave one last sneeze, touched my hat's pansies and started out quietly:

"We want President Roosevelt to hear the wail of the children who never have a chance to go to school." I looked up at the riveted crowd; flanking it, I noticed, were those same burly, grim men in dark suits. Their gaze was keen and trained on me.

I took a breath and went on. "These children work eleven and twelve hours a day in the textile mills. They weave the carpets that you and the President stand on. They make the lace curtains that hang in your windows — and the clothes of the people."

Again, I looked up; the Secret Service agents had moved closer. I knew I couldn't let them distract me again. If they took me into custody, I'd go out speaking at the top of my voice. I forced myself to go on.

"In Georgia, where children work night and day in the cotton mills, they just passed a law to protect song birds." I paused to let that sink in. "Song birds, you heard me. What about the little children from whom all song is gone?"

The crowd looked stunned until I finished speaking, and the next day the scene was all over the papers. Interest in the marchers seemed to be building once again. The timing was right. That afternoon, with three of the boys, I took the train out of the city to Sagamore Hills and President Roosevelt.

I had selected Jim Ashcroft and two of his friends with careful thought. Just now, it would be a mistake to

present myself as the head of some populist army. I
wanted to look like a grandmother, bringing her boys on
a cordial visit. We must not upset the Secret Service.
Still, I wondered what kind of harm they thought I might
do. What I wanted was Roosevelt's mercy. With his
backing, a bill could go to Congress, enacting a Federal
law against child labor. That was all I came to say.

Before we could reach the gates of the President's
mansion, we were stopped by four men — the same ones
who had followed us through half the march. They
loomed above us, those strapping, serious guards, and I
could see the bulge of firearms under their suits. The
leader of this Secret Service stepped forward. His
message, delivered in a menacing voice, was simple and
terse: The President had refused to see us.

~~

As we walked down the great drive, I threw an arm over
the boys. They said nothing but their stooped shoulders
seemed to sag even more. Up till that final rejection, I
think, they truly believed that they would meet their
President.

I'd warned them that this might not come to be; I'd
warned myself dozens of times. Still, the sting of that
snub did not seem to leave us. I remember the silence. I
remember the date. It was the Twenty-Ninth of July and
we had been on the road for three weeks. We rode up in
the elevator to the room we shared in a cheap hotel near
Times Square.

"Never mind," I said brightly. "I'll write him one more
time."

"But Mother — he must think we're trash," Jimmy
said.

"That you're not, d'ya hear me?" I flinched at his
words.

"Would he answer a letter this time?"

"I think he will." I tried to sound certain.

As soon as the letter was done and the ink was dry, I read it aloud.

"Mr. President," it began. "The child of today is the man or woman of tomorrow. I have with me three children who have walked one hundred miles. If you decide to see these children, I will bring them before you at any time you may set." I signed the letter and sent it off. The reply was so fast, it seemed as if my letter had been expected. The boys grew excited but I noted the way the envelope looked. This was a response from the President's office, not Roosevelt himself. I felt an inner sinking as I opened the letter; as I read it, the boys hung over my shoulder.

"This comes from the President's secretary," I told them at last; then I took a breath. "President Roosevelt wishes to convey his opinion: Child labor, he believes, is a problem for the each state to resolve." I looked up. "That's all it says. I'm sorry, boys. You gave it such a grand try."

"I thought he was a good guy," Jim Ashcroft said after a while.

"He's a brave guy when he wants to take a gun out and fight other grown people." I could not keep the bitterness out of my voice. "But when children come to him, he can't see them."

Even for a moment, I thought.

Even for a handshake.

I stood up and stared at the cracks on the wall of this tawdry room. There was no longer any point to staying in New York City. I only hoped that the mill children would return to a strike that had held firm.

I took the boys home to Kensington, Pennsylvania. When we got off the train, we lingered together for a few minutes on the platform. I gathered the boys into a quick embrace, then sent them off to their homes. I was too tired to get back on the train; I stayed the night in a rooming house near the depot.

And so, I was there, the next day, when the strike fell apart and the workers went back to the mill, taking their children with them. The strike had yielded no progress at all. Nothing was gained in wages or hours, or working conditions.

Purely by reflex I got back on the train, heading for Scranton, where the Powderlys lived. As the car swayed, I laid my head on the back of my seat. I wondered how the children would do at the mill, after their brief taste of freedom. Would this month shine in their minds as a magical season — or would they recall it with resentment and anger? Would they dream of the sea and the stars, the open fields, the nightly circle around the cooking pot? Or would they blot it all from their minds forever? Still worse, I wondered if the bosses would punish the returning marchers.

I could not know — I never did.

By the time I arrived at the Powderlys' home, my hands were trembling and my hair had come down. Emma and Terence welcomed me as family, but I could not eat my supper, even in that calm, lamplit house. In the dining room, the polished floors shone and a tall clock ticked and chimed. Murmuring apologies, I pushed back my plate. Then I put my head down on the table and wept.

"You're exhausted," said Emma. "Just plain worn out."

"Children, Mary," Terence said. "Pretty tough for you."

"Pretty brave, I'd say." Emma smoothed my hair.

"I've lost strikes before." I looked up at them.

"Not this kind," Terence said quietly.

"Did I do harm?" My voice rose, then cracked.

"You gave them a window onto the world," Emma said.

"But what good did I do?" My voice rose again.

"You can't know yet," Terence said. "Wait, Mary. Wait."

"And rest." A frown creased Emma's pretty face.

There was a long pause.

"Oh, damn it to hell," I burst out finally.

"She's on the mend," Terence winked at Emma.

Terence was right. Just then, I didn't realize the mighty impact of "The Mill Children's March." For a long while to come, it made big headlines in all major papers, and the march itself became a legend of sorts. That ragtag army somehow caught the public's imagination and the subject of child labor began to command national attention. Within five years of the march, New York, New Jersey, and Pennsylvania had passed legislation to tighten their states' child labor laws. There is still so much to be overcome. I continue to hope for that Federal action we'd tried to win — now, at least, I believe it will happen one of these days.

Wait, Terence advised. I did; I still do.

Rest, Emma urged. I didn't do that.

Not that she really expected it, knowing me.

Soon I was off on other trains, to other strikes.

~~

Even so, I still dreamed of Jim Ashcroft, now and then, along with my own daughters and son. I dreamed of all the mill children from time to time.

Like my shoes and my address, their faces came with me wherever I went.

■

« 15 »

Aand so, I went on.

But I never did forgive that President.

Later, I testified before Congress about the lives of mill children and that summer march. There, in the Senate chambers, I faced a row of well-tailored men, well-groomed men. Ranged behind a long table, they studied me with a mix of respect and curiosity. I did not need to study them. I'd formed my opinion of such types long before. Once, I met a man who's been jailed for stealing a pair of shoes. I told him that if he'd stolen a railroad, he'd be a United States Senator. Clearly, though, this was not a good time to repeat this particular interchange. I only looked up at the inquisitors before me. One of the men had a moustache like Roosevelt's; I saw it and felt my old fury rise up against him, all over again.

I was asked to describe our "interaction or lack thereof."

"He had a lot of Secret Service men watching an old woman and an army of children." I could not keep the disgust from my voice. "You fellows do elect wonderful presidents. The best thing you can do is put a woman in there next time."

To a man, that Senate Committee stared at me.

Over my spectacles, I stared right back.

"Women decide the fate of a nation," I added.

One of them spoke words I'll not gorget: "You're the grandmother of all agitators."

"I hope. I'd love to be their great-grandmother," I snapped.

~~

Up in Milwaukee, I spoke to group of female workers.

"Women are fighters," I told them that night.

"*Yes*," the audience shouted. "Yes" — and "*Si*."

"They are the inner life of the human race, every drop of their blood precious." I looked out at the packed hall before me. "As soon as every woman grasps the idea that every other woman is her sister, then we will begin to better conditions."

Stepping down from the box where I'd stood, I opened my arms and called them all, "sister." They repeated that word, as they drew close to me. Soon they were chanting, "Sister, sister," though many of them were new immigrants, with little English at their command. What a grand mix of women crowded that room: Italians, Greeks, Slavs, Irish, and native-born girls — all of them single and self-supporting. If they didn't know the word, "Sister," they learned it that night. They already well knew at least two more English words. These went together. The words were, "*No Fair*."

I'd been called to Milwaukee to organize women who labored long hours in beer factories. Their numbers were not as big as the miners, but their cause was very important to me. All through my labor career, I'd admired the strength and grit of the women I'd met — from the "Mop and Broom Army" in Arnot, Pennsylvania, to Delia Smith, fleeing her Southern mill. Now it was time to give more attention to these female workers, overlooked until now.

I always like to take a couple of months and study the facts before I go into a field. What I learned about these women's working conditions was shocking, to say the least. I was engaged — and enraged, I might add. As always, I thought of my daughters. They might have grown up to labor just like these young girls. And who would help them?

The plight of women, like that of children, was often forgotten or set aside. I saw this happen many times: men's causes, like mining, were more dramatic and to many, more pressing than these bottle-washers here in Milwaukee. These working girls thought otherwise.

I shared a room with two of the girls in another drab company shack. There, I immersed myself in the facts of their lives, and the more I learned, my anger increased. Clearly, the brewery owners, like the mill bosses, exploited these women — just because they could make money on them. Here were the figures, right before me.

Beer factories paid sweat-shop wages: Seventy-five cents a day; eighty, at most. The girls told me that their pay hardly covered their room and board. They were paid just enough to keep them alive and on the job. Not so easy in winter, when I was with them, there in the snows of Wisconsin.

For these girls had no money to purchase warm clothing; a ride on a streetcar was a rare treat. To get to their factories, I trudged with the girls across icy pavements and through snowy streets. I still had my hip boots from West Virginia, but these girls had flimsy wet shoes that never dried as the work day went on.

With a shawl tied over my hair, I managed to slip through the factory gates. Once inside, I could observe the breweries' working conditions first-hand. These were worse than I had expected:

For less than five dollars a week, the girls washed beer bottles in damp, dingy rooms, where it was easy to slip on the floors, always covered with dirty water. In addition to this, the women had to lift cases of bottles, empty and full, weighing up to 150 pounds. Most of the girls weighed far less than those cases they heaved into the air. Their backs ached; their bones ached. Many looked older than they were.

I shivered inside those factories, wondering how many workers would come down with pneumonia. "Oh, *molto* pneumonia, *Si*," an Italian girl nodded. Another English word she had already learned. "*No finito*," she said at the end of the day. She pushed her dark hair back and led me to the factory lunchroom. This she had to clean "*Adesso*" — now — while other girls worked mopping up other rooms, for no extra pay. In her halting English, Caterina told me how closely the boss kept his eyes on them.

"*Sempre*," she said, glancing over her shoulder.

"*Sempre*?" I asked for a translation.

"Always he watch," Caterina whispered.

"He wants you to work all the time?"

"*Si*," she nodded. "'*Bagno* time, too."

"He clocks you for using the bathroom?"

Nodding again, Caterina took my cold hand.

"I come to America for better," she sighed.

"We'll try for better," I promised that night.

~~

After I visited the Blatz Brewery, I saw a fight lay ahead.

In the paneled vestibule, I was kept waiting for a long time.

Then a door swung open and a secretary led me into the "executive wing." There, a heavy, flushed man greeted me at his office door. To my surprise, Mr. Blatz offered his paw-like hand. It was large and moist.

"How do you do?" we both uttered the niceties at once.

I remember my heels sinking into plush carpet. I remember the sight of Blatz squeezing behind his mahogany desk. I remember he lit up a fat cigar and blew smoke-rings at the ceiling.

"Now then, Mrs. Jones, what's on your mind?"

"Your female employees." I came to the point.

"Why? You the grandma to one of them gals?"

"Well, I am and I'm not —" A handy Irish phrase.

"What the hell does *that* mean, Mrs. Jones?"

"Your plant needs a union now, Mr. Blatz."

"You're joking. *A union?*" He stared at me.

" You heard me. A union. Sure, that's no joke."

"You one of them Mick troublemakers?"

I hated Blatz for that, but I thought of the girls.

"I'm a labor organizer," I said, holding back.

"You? Think you can jerk me around?"

"Lock me out and I'll go to the statehouse."

"You do that, little lady. Be my guest."

Clearly, the interview had come to an end.

At the door, I turned for one parting shot.

"'Mick' is a man's name — not a nationality."

His eyes on me, Blatz used the spittoon.

"You'd damn well better remember," I hissed.

Still glaring, I slammed the door after me.

Outside in the street, the cold was biting and the wind was high — but I was still heated up from that meeting. From Blatz's comments, I figured the brewers had some tight pals at the statehouse in Madison. This was the same story I'd heard in West Virginia — here, too, the bosses' cronies were judges.

For a moment, I just stood there in the street, trying to think what to do. An idea edged forward, like a friend finding you in the midst of a crowd. I wouldn't bother with lawmakers or judges, then. I'd go where I had some cronies, myself.

~~

My cronies did not inhabit paneled, plush offices.

I was in tight with a far different crowd — the ones who spent six days a week underground. Every mining camp, I well knew, had a saloon — Dolly's or Polly's or Sal's, they were all pretty much the same. In these saloons, workers could slouch in their chairs and knock back a drink to blunt the day's labor. With the boys, I'd downed some brew, myself, now and then.

Sometimes, I wonder if that's one of the things that clinched our connection. The miners knew I cared about them, that was sure, but they also knew I could share in their ways. Mother Jones was no Lady Bountiful from Fifth Avenue, that much was plain.

The first time I went to a miner's saloon was near Pittsburgh and the place was called Dolly's. The bartender, Dolly herself, stared at me, along with the men. She had a pretty, worn face, I remember, touched up with rouge. She pushed back her yellow hair as I came in.

There, in my black dress and black hat and spectacles, I called for a pint and a shot. As I swallowed them both, the saloon fell totally silent. Someone positioned a stool right behind me, in case I passed out. My skirts rustled as I swept past it to shake Dolly's hand. Behind her was a line of miners, waiting to shake mine. Now, in this fight for the Milwaukee girls, I thought I might draw on that powerful bond.

That week, it just so happened that Cincinnati was hosting a national gathering of union boys. For months, I'd been planning to attend. Now I hopped a train and headed for the annual United Mine Workers Convention. I can't recall the hotel where it was; I can't recall much of hilly Cincinnati. I was too busy moving among the convention's many delegates, with a very specific request. I knew this would involve some sacrifice — I also knew the boys would understand.

Milwaukee supplied most of the mining camps' beer. My request was simple: Boycott all beer made in Milwaukee. And I told the men that together, we'd give the brewers the damnedest fight they'd ever had. Men slapped my back and shook on their promise. Then they quickly passed the word around. There was unanimous agreement; I knew the mining community would come through.

One of the boys noted that I was looking well. "Of course I am," I told him. "There's going to be a racket and I'm going to be in it. When I get a lick at them, it makes me young again."

Our plan would not have the same effect on Mr. Blatz, I figured. With his fellow brewers, he'd soon be hurting badly. This was no ladylike gesture — or even a shot at a spittoon. I wished I could be there when Blatz got the word: Five hundred thousand miners would boycott Milwaukee's brews, his included.

When this news reached Wisconsin, in short order, it buzzed quickly throughout the beer industry. I imagined those brewery owners denting each other's plush carpet as meetings were held on short notice. The UMW backed the boycott and the big beer kingpins saw millions of dollars foaming away. This was no empty threat, they soon realized. I wondered if Blatz had run out of cigars. It didn't take long for those Milwaukee brewers to give it up and cave in.

I was with the bottle-washers, the day that they voted in their union. They wept, they cheered, they embraced each other. Forming a line, they held out their hands to receive their union cards. Then the girls gathered around me. One of them shouted "Sister" and soon, the room filled with that word, chanted and sung out and shouted in five different languages.

After the celebration, I had to move on once again, but I kept up with Caterina and many others. They wasted no time and ran their union efficiently. They had a new sense of pride – and they recalled my advice: "Whatever the fight, don't be ladylike." Soon, they had won higher wages and improvements in their working conditions.

"*Molto Grazie*," Caterina telegraphed to me.

Before I left Milwaukee, I stopped in at the offices of Mr. Blatz.

"Do you have an appointment, Ma'am?" The secretary eyed me.

"Just tell Mr. Blatz it's the Mick from the union," I told her.

I left him a green shamrock: "For luck — he'll need it."

Smiling sweetly, I adjusted my hat and let myself out.

■

Outside my jail cell, that priest still hovers.
"You believe in luck?" he asks me now.
"I do and I don't." Why is he here at the jail?
"You trust in God?" The priest squints at me.
"I don't and I do." That should confuse him.
"My mother said that." He smiles abruptly.
"Father," I sigh. "Why are you here?"
"In case you wanted to make a confession."
"To what?" I explode. "What have I done?"
"You're a Socialist, aren't you?" He squints again.
"If you like. I've been called other things, too."
"You helped found the Industrial Workers of the World?"
"I did — but I quit. You think I'm a sinner for that?"
"Do you still believe in God, Mary Jones?"
"I do — what is this, the Spanish Inquisition?"
"You don't seem to think much of the clergy."
"Nothing personal. Just the folks I call 'sky-pilots.'"
"The ones promising 'pie in the sky when you die?' "
"Father, some tell workers to bear exploitation."

"The Church..." He sighs. "A human institution."

"We agree on that one." There is an odd lengthy silence.

"Am I sentenced to hang?" Suddenly, I'm on alert.

"I doubt it. Did you want the Last Rites?"

"Not today, thank you....someday, though."

"You say that swearing can be likened to prayer?"

"Damn right, Father." I grin as he shakes his head.

"You do much good, Mrs. Jones, all the same."

"The prodigal daughter — Father, thank you."

"God bless you, my child, and your dear departed."

After he leaves I still see his carroty hair, his pale gray eyes, the cleft in his chin. I still hear his parting words to me, as well. I wish he had not mentioned my dear departed. He must not realize how that pain stays on, no matter how busy or feisty I seem. "Feisty" — that's the press's new word for me. This week. Last week, General Chase — Governor Ammons' attack dog — called me "a hag." The week before, he called me a "witch." I've called him some words that the papers would not print. Maybe Chase, to harass me, sent that priest here to my cell here in Colorado.

Prison, as I've said, is not new to me.

Long ago, Eugene Debs told me, it comes with the calling. I keep the UMWA's lawyers fairly busy — not that I'm the only one who gets into fixes. I'm grateful to be with this Union again. There were a few years when we parted ways; Johnny Mitchell and I had a falling-out.

"Goddamn it, Mother," he began.

"Goddamn it, Son," I'd snap back.

It sounded like a family quarrel.

In fact, so it was.

And a serious one, too.

John Mitchell had wanted a negotiated settlement in an earlier Colorado mining strike. He told the northern miners to go back to work; I told them to fight on, in support of their brothers in Southern Colorado. In the end, the state split in half — something I'd worked to prevent — and Mitchell was enraged at me.

"How dare you?" he hollered.

"I did what I thought was right."

"You went against my orders."

"You weren't there in the field."

"That's no excuse, Mother."

"Son, it's an explanation."

"It's a damn accusation."

"It damn well is not."

"You think I sold out," his voice rose.

"Oh, Yes," I flared up. "Fire me, then."

"You can't tell me what to do."

"You're not my boss — you're a king now.?

"Mother, with all due respect — go to hell."

"See you there. Meanwhile, I quit."

We did not speak for a while and I went to work for the Western Federation of Miners. I guess that was more than a quarrel, it was a breaking point. It's a sorrow to me that our friendship never really recovered. Johnny Mitchell always seemed like a son to me. If my children had lived, they would have been close to his age. His parents were poor Irish immigrants like mine, though his people went to the Illinois coal fields for work.

I have to hand it to Johnny: he went to work in the mines at thirteen to help support his stepmother, his brothers and sisters. He was only fifteen when he joined the Knights of Labor and I often wondered if I'd seen him at those early meetings. I knew him as a founding member and soon, president, of the United Mine Workers.

I will always be grateful to him for hiring me on as a paid organizer — but I knew we would end up at odds. I always thought he was too quick to give in to the mine owners; too quick to negotiate. I shouldn't judge, I know, but he did live a damn luxurious life for someone in his position.   Still, I have to admit, Johnny Mitchell did accomplish a great deal for the union, until he was forced out around 1909, I believe that was. I'm thankful to Tom Lewis, who took his place — and hired me back on to work with the miners once again.

~~

I always knew I'd come back to West Virginia.

I just hadn't known I'd come back to disaster.

Ten years earlier, we had worked so hard there and risked a great deal. Now, much of our unionizing had come undone, especially south of the Kenawah River. Once again, coal-fields were strike zones.   Forty companies had brought in strikebreakers — and hired "guards" to protect them. In reality, these "guards" were paid thugs from the Baldwin-Felts Detective Agency.

I was out in Montana when I heard about West Virginia's flare-up. The situation, I heard, was explosive and could get bloody. Thousands of coal miners had walked off their jobs — and they were asking for me. I cancelled my San Francisco lecture series and caught an express train speeding East. Abruptly, I'd ended my longest streak of cross-country traveling.

There was an certain urgency to my work at that time. Throughout my seventies, I tried to do as much as I could while I was still blessed with health and staying power. I had taken on several new challenges: I'd stood with telegraph operators in Chicago and silk-weavers in Pennsylvania. I'd sat with girls who sewed shirtwaists in New York and boys who mined copper in Arizona. In Minnesota, I'd fought for the rights of iron ore workers — and that assignment nearly undid me.

Every blackened face made me think of my husband. Every day, I learned more about what he'd done — on ten and twelve hour stretches. This he'd done for us: his family. I recalled how George had to keep working throughout the plague. He'd had no choice; if he didn't work, he'd lose his job. Strenuous hot work it was, too, and I now believed that it had worn him down till he couldn't fight the Yellow Fever. All these years later, I felt his loss as if it were new, and this time the pain was mixed with fresh rage.

When I got off the train in Charleston, West Virginia, I was still angry about the past. Soon enough, I was angry about the present, as well. Organizers met me at the depot and explained what we faced. In Paint Creek, union miners had gone out on strike to protest their new contract: it did not answer the miners' demands for improved working conditions.

That was only one bad situation. At Cabin Creek, the local miners had not been unionized and they were to stand with the Paint Creek men. These two small towns, with their quaint names, lay at opposite ends of a long ravine. This area was patrolled by heavily armed "guards," courtesy of Baldwin-Felts. So far, they'd been able to keep organizers out of the region. I was furious when I was warned against interference there. Even the union boys told me I'd come out of that ravine on a stretcher.

All right, I thought, grimly this time.

Here we go — once again.

Damn it.

My first move was a trip to Eskdale, another small town that was free of coal operators. I used this town as a base for a while. Railroad friends spread the word that Eskdale would host my first "return speech" in Eskdale. It was a risk, I knew, but well worth it. Miners came from both Paint Creek and Cabin Creek, despite hard feelings between the two areas.

Yes – I was already angry when I got off the train — and grew angrier still when I found West Virginia in turmoil again. That might explain why I took a new stand in that first speech. For the first time in my life, I encouraged the men to consider fighting violence with violence. The coal operators erupted when they heard of my talk. Ignoring them, I printed up leaflets and had them distributed to the non-union Cabin Creek men. "In the name of the outraged women and murdered miners of Paint Creek, I beseech you to lay down your tools and join your striking brothers."

A confrontation was bound to come soon.

In fact, it came the next day. I had just organized another march to Red Warrior, West Virginia. This time, dozens of Paint Creek miners tramped down the road in a peaceful line. We were heading toward a coal camp to see if the Cabin Creek miners would join force with us. Leading the marchers, I drove a one-horse buggy through that hot summer day, while dust swirled on the road and the leaves wilted on withered trees.

In the distance, through the shimmering heat, I spotted some figures moving in our direction. Maybe they were miners trying to join us; then again, maybe not. At a quick pace, the figures drew nearer. Quickly then, they came into focus. They were armed mine guards, fifty strong, and I caught the glimmer of sun on their machine guns. The men behind me slowed down, then halted.

For what seemed a long time our boys stared at the guards; they gazed back, eyes narrowed, aiming their machine guns at us. From the side of the road, I heard the humming of insects — that was all. I surveyed the scene, trying to get a sense of the guards' resolve. The chance of a bloodbath seemed high; too high. I realized that we were on the edge of a losing battle.

I stepped down from the buggy.

No one spoke a word on either side.

Slowly, deliberately, I walked toward the guards' leader. He eyed me, keeping one finger near his gun's trigger. Clearly, I was not part of his plan. When I finally spoke, my voice sounded distant to me — and a bit like a strict schoolmarm's, I thought, scolding a pupil. I reached out and wrapped my hand around the gun's muzzle.

"Listen, you," I snapped out the words. "Up there in the mountain, I have eight hundred armed miners. They're marching to join the meeting I'm going to address. You fire one shot and they won't leave one of your gang alive."

A silence drew itself out, taut as a clothesline.

Then, jerking his head, the leader signaled his men to stand aside.

I climbed back onto the buggy and our men marched on — though, of course, there were no armed miners up in the hills. But no blood was shed, that summer day.

As I've often said, I have a preference for drama.

~~

Soon enough, we got more than drama.

This was a shock; we had made gains. Cabin Creek miners joined forces with Paint Creek men: at last, a victory for us and one that hit the coal companies hard. To keep up things rolling, I went to speak in Charleston, West Virginia. The audience gathered on the Capitol's steps as I stood up, as tall as I could. I gave the miners some fire, this time.

"Get rid of mine guards forever," I called out.

The crowd cheered; the police looked on.

"One day," I added, "you will run your own mines."

More cheers. More police circling.

"Can't you just hear the coal operators now?" I demanded. "Oh, them horrible miners! That horrible woman, that Mother Jones. Well, let them call us names! After all, their wives wear five dollars worth of makeup and have toothbrushes for their *dogs*...."

A swell of laughter broke from the audience.

"Listen to me now." My voice quieted. "Never be afraid, my friends. Fear is a terrible enemy. Join me, at old lady, and fear no one. I tell you all, the day of oppression be over. Instead of the horrible homes you have, we will build on their ruins — good homes for you and your children to live in."
Silence, now. I held out my hands.
"I will be with you whether true or false. I will be with you at midnight — or when the battle rages. When the last bullet ceases to fly, I will be in my joy. As an old saint sang out:
'Oh God of the mighty clan,
God grant that the woman who suffered for you,
Suffered not for a coward, but oh, for a man.
God grant that the woman who suffered for you,
Suffered not for a coward, but oh, for a fighting man.'"
I saw tears on the faces before me, as the cheers rose. Suddenly, an old man pushed his way through the crowd, his eyes fixed on me. As his hand darted to his pocket, the boys behind me quickly stepped forward. No one doubted that there were guns in this gathering. The man's white hair seemed to smoke from his head and there was blue fire in his eyes. Shaking off all restraints, he ran straight at me. I did not move; I knew I could not show fear now. The man reached into his pocket — and drew out a ten dollar bill.
"Take this," he said, "and shake hands with me, an old union miner."
My eyes filled; I can still feel his rough palm against mine.
Then the man turned to the crowd.
"Fight, fight, right," he shouted. "I'm union — my children can take care of themselves and I will take care of myself. I have a good rifle and I'll get more money. If I don't have enough to pay my railroad fare, I'll walk. I

don't care if this was the last cent I had, I will give it to 'Mother' and go get some more."

My team of organizers, seizing this moment, passed an old hat. We turned the donations over to the miners and soon, I read about this speech in the papers. "Head and shoulders above all the other agitators in ability and forcefulness stands 'Mother Jones,' the heroine of many strikes," wrote Larry Lynch. And what a fine boy he must be. "She knows no fear and is as much at home in jail as on the platform. In either situation, she wields a greater power over the miners than does any other agitator."

Of course, it was pleasing to read Lynch's words. But I knew the coal operators were reading them, too, and there would be a bloody backlash against us. I sent a petition up to the statehouse, calling on Governor Glasscock to stop the armed guards. The governor, I well knew, was a coward and wouldn't reply. I'd had enough of elected officials who turned needy folks away. And I hated the forces that drove us to threaten violence. Clearly, in West Virginia, we were on our own — no one would protect us from what was to come.

"We will protect ourselves," I told the miners. "We will buy every gun here in Charleston."

And so the men did. As I watched them that day, I thought of the Minute Men in New England, marching up the creeks to their homes, with the grimness of the soldiers of the revolution. Soon afterwards, that summer of 1912, union miners lined the Kenawah River and waded across it to support the miners of Cabin Creek. The coal operators sent for more armed guards and called up employees with rifles on hand. The armed camps faced one another. I knew what was coming — this would be war.

I guess the governor knew that, as well. In September, he imposed martial law on the strike zone. A great terror ran through the valley as soldiers ransacked people's homes, confiscating all weapons, all ammunition. Grimly, I kept speaking out. As I expected, I was stopped and "detained" in a railway depot; my "crime" was reading the Declaration of Independence to a crowd of miners.

Still, I knew we had to keep spirits high, so I found some banners and a brass band. The banners may have been tattered and worn; the band's brass may have sounded off-key. Nonetheless, they drew a crowd as I led miners' children on a march through the city of Charleston. It was only a stopgap measure, I knew, though the soldiers left Charleston in October. There was a short and tense truce. I gave it a month. That's what we got. In November, the mine owners imported trainloads of scabs. No mops or brooms could intervene now. The Kenawah strikers met the trains with firepower. Once again, martial law was declared in the strike zone.

I began to wonder if West Virginia was still part of America.

It was starting to feel more like Ireland to me.

I went on the road to publicize new abuses:

"This is an outrage," I told a group in Ohio. "A military tribunal has taken over the legal system in West Virginia. The civil courts stand empty Out the window go basics rights: to counsel, to take the Fifth Amendment, and more. The tribunal now arrests people outside the strike zone. Where will this end? Is anyone listening?"

In the end, it wasn't words that drew attention.

Once again, it was violence.

~~

I will always remember Holly Grove.

There, on a bitter February day, striking miners huddled with their families in a tent colony — their former "landlords," the coal companies, had put them out of their homes. As they cooked their noon meal, a special train, bearing mounted machine guns, sped toward that tent colony, called Holly Grove. There, the guards opened fire on the camp.

When I heard the news, I remember, I sat down hard and tried to imagine the scene: blazing guns riddling tent canvas; tin plates of stew overturned as people dropped to the ground. I tried not to think about screaming babies and stampeding mothers. There were casualties — and unnumbered children were terrorized. Then came retaliation: Enraged miners fired on the guards' headquarters at Mucklow. Soon, martial law was declared once again.

The strikers begged me to bring their cause before the governor. I was hardly his favorite person, I knew, but someone had to speak for the embattled miners. Carefully, I selected a party of thirty-four cool-headed men, and with them, I took another train back to the state capital, Charleston. We carried printed protest resolutions; no guns, no kind of arms.

As we left the Charleston station, we marched peacefully to the statehouse. There we were stopped. I was seized. Detained. And suddenly shoved into a waiting automobile. Before I could glance out the window, the car sped away. I was stunned; I was furious. I was told to keep quiet. I looked into the muzzle of another machine gun. This time it seemed wise to keep my hands to myself.

When I reached military headquarters at Pratt, I learned what had happened. Some unknown enemy had sent a "riot call" out to the governor. It was a false warning, of course, and an absurd one, describing me as the leader of 3,500 armed men. Our alleged mission: to assassinate the governor and blow up the capitol. To this day, I flush with rage as I think of this dirty insult, this wild accusation. Trouble was, the militia believed it.

The charges against me were these:

Theft of a machine gun.

Conspiracy to murder.

Attempt to blow up a train.

That was it.

That was enough.

In short order, I was locked up tight. My jail was a shack in the town of Pratt, and I was kept there in strict solitary confinement. I was permitted no newspapers, no correspondence, no conversation with anyone. Of course, it wasn't too hard to get around this. There were quiet union sympathizers who had escaped the latest dragnet. My jailors were kindly and I did not hesitate to bribe them.

Soon I was smuggling letters out of the place I called, "The Military Bastille." We had a system, my jailors and I. There was a hole in the floor of my prison, where I would stash letters. When I gave a signal, the jailors crawled under the floorboards and retrieved the letters, already addressed, and saw to it they got into the mail. Nice boys, those jailors; I still recall the glint of high adventure in their young eyes.

~~

In the military courtroom, I refused to enter a plea.

In fact, I refused to recognize the court's authority at all.

I was accused of actions that never took place, but if they had, they would have been before martial law was declared. I'd not been arrested, to my way of thinking, I'd damn well been kidnaped — and outside the strike zone, as well. Only there did martial law rule. I understood my rights well enough: If I were to be tried, it should be in a civil court. I'd been given no hearing, no grand grand-jury's indictment — and I damn well protested.

After receiving my daily letters, the state's attorney general came to see me in jail. He was not responsive to my rendition of these abuses; he just stared at me as if I were a curiosity at a fairgrounds. Then he noted that my crimes carried with them the death penalty, carried out military style: by firing squad.

Once again, I lost my temper.

"Tell this to the governor," I burst out. "He can chain me up to that tree outside and he can get his dogs of war to riddle this body with bullets — but I won't surrender my constitutional rights to him. I happen to be one of those women who tramped the highways where revolutionists' blood watered it, so I might have trial by jury."

Without a word, the attorney left.

On my behalf, union attorneys filed a petition with the state's Supreme Court. This verdict was handed down: under a state of war, West Virginia had the right to detain me and others, in light of the "public danger" we posed. Judge Ira E. Robinson dissented strongly, writing that "this State is a land of constitutional courts, not one of imperial military courts. A dispute between mine owners and miners cannot be considered public war and the participants dealt with as enemies of the state."

I'll always bless Judge Robinson for his spirited defense, but in the end, nothing changed for me — except my health. No one else was surprised, but I was. I'd counted on my own strength and it began to break down. In that shack on the Kenawah River, I grew short of breath. My face seemed to blaze, though I shook with chills. Soon I was flat-out on a straw pallet — and there I was, still, when a new governor was inaugurated in Charleston. I worsened — and wondered if I was going to die there, in that shack. After a while, I was too sick to think about anything, except my next labored breath.

Finally, through a haze, I looked up at a stranger. His face hung like a lantern above me. For a moment, I thought the firing squad had come to get me at last. Then I noticed the doctor's bag in this man's hand. As he examined me, he spoke out loud in a brisk voice:

"Temperature, one hundred and four degrees....very rapid respiration....a constant cough...pneumonia..."

Before I could speak, I was lifted from the pallet and, on doctor's orders, taken to Charleston for treatment. It was only then that I learned that this doctor was none other than Henry D. Hatfield, the new governor of West Virginia. Imagine: A labor agitator's life had been saved — by a Republican.

Hatfield was visiting the strike zone when he came to see me. By all accounts, he understood the miners' position. While he was still in medical practice, he had started up three hospitals for them and their families. Still, he had the support of the mine operators; it was they who had helped Hatfield get into office. And once I'd recovered somewhat, the good doctor sent me back to jail.

That spring, I heard rumors of a Senate investigation of West Virginia's ongoing troubles. I asked my jailors to keep me informed and from them I learned that Indiana's Senator John W. Kern, had submitted a resolution to start such an inquiry. Always pro-labor, I knew, Kern wanted to learn if strikers' civil rights had been violated.

It was the first of May, my adopted birthday — and my seventy-sixth — when I decided to smuggle a telegram out to the Senator. It reached him and shortly thereafter, Kern read my words on the Senate floor and into the Congressional record. My father's Ribbonboys would have been proud.

"I plead with you for the honor of this nation," I wrote. "I send you groans and tears of men, women and children as I have heard in this state, and beg you to force that investigation. Children yet unborn will rise up and bless you...."

Kern picked up support — and opposition. Naturally, this was led by one Nathan Goff, a senator from West Virginia; where else? Goff favored the mine owners and branded me as a destructive outsider, inciting riot and urging insurrection.

My jailor read those words to me from the papers.

"I'm sorry, Mother. Goff is no good."

"He's not a bad fellow," I remarked. "He's just been dead forty years and doesn't know it."

At least I gave my jailors a laugh.

I could not quite laugh, myself.

Meanwhile, Kern stood firm on the floor of the Senate. "I am appalled," he said, "that 300 miles from Washington, one of the best known women in America...has been tried in this unusual way before this mock tribunal." Kern was shocked, he added, that the press had not reported my situation — nor had Hatfield made my court-martial known. "Whether this old woman is to die or live," added Senator Kern, "whether she is to spend the rest of her life in prison or go free is known only to the one man who sets his will above the law of the land."

Hatfield shot back. The governor declared that I was not in prison. I was only "detained," he insisted, in a "pleasant boarding house." That was one hell of a whopper. In any event, Kern's resolution held its own on the Senate floor, and the debate raged on.

One morning, expecting a smuggled newspaper, I heard my cell door's bolt shoot open. Then the door itself swung wide. I rose to my feet, expecting the worst, but my young guards were grinning at me. Embarrassed by Kern and the public outcry, Governor Hatfield had released me — after eighty-five days, locked up at Pratt.

Soon, I was in Washington sitting up in the Senate gallery, watching that good man, John W. Kern, continue his fight, and on the twenty-seventh of May, his resolution finally passed.

The resulting investigation did find that civil rights had been disregarded and abused. New state legislation was on it way. I tried to find words to express this to the miners: "We won't allow military despotism in America," I told them, as soon as we could meet together. The miners cheered; we all wiped our eyes.

"They said I'd come out of here on a stretcher," I noted.

"God forbid that," voices called out to me from the crowd.

"I didn't come out on a stretcher," I lifted my fist. "I raised hell."

~~

I remember when I left West Virginia.

Looking up at the capitol in Charleston, I knew that much of this state had changed for good. Fifty brave people had died in the coal wars: martyrs, whose blood watered the hillsides — and flowed into freer lives for so many. The striking miners finally won an eight-hour work day and their own weigh-men at the check-out scales.

The United Mine Workers of America gained almost 5,000 new members in the state. Organizers were already working with miners in the New River area and within two years, that region, too, went for the union. The dreaded mine-guard system was put to an end. I have lived to see the unionization of half the state's miners. As I write, the southern edge of West Virginia is still to be won.

"We shall go on." That was my constant promise.

I remember making that promise one night in New York City.

That night, I took the stage at Carnegie Hall.

Here, the greatest artists had performed for people of every class. The very walls seemed steeped in music. Maybe this occasion called for a gown of green silk — but I wore my widow's black dress.

I stepped up to the rostrum. I gazed out over the sold-out crowd. There was a stillness in the hall and again, I could sense the music that was played there for millions. The only notes I could add were made of words.

"We shall go on," I told the audience, once more.

I gazed around once again and opened my hands.

"God commanded the prophets, thousands of years ago, to free the people. God commanded Moses to break the Israelites' oppression and lead God's people out of bondage. And they went up out of Egypt and crossed the Red Sea; and their pursuers were stopped in their chase. God fed the people in the wilderness and so too, today's people must be fed."

I looked over my spectacles at the uplifted faces. "Believe in yourselves now and forever. No boss, no minister, no official will change our lives for the better. We, the people — we've got to do it."

I saw people leaning forward, attentive and still.

"We have fought together, we have hungered together, we have marched together, but I see victory for you. I can see the hand above you guiding and inspiring you to move onward and upward. The star that rose over Bethlehem, long ago, has crossed the world. It has risen here. See it slowly breaking through the crowds? The star of Bethlehem will usher in the new day and new time — and if you are true, you will be free...."

In that grand hall, a swell of applause rose and grew louder and still it rose, higher and higher. I stood in silence, there where concert pianos made music.

What did the crowd hear? That night, I wondered.

The voice of an old woman in black?

They heard the voice of my father, Richard Harris.

The voice of my husband, George Jones.

The voices of my children, so many children now.

The voices from the mills and the mines and the marches.

They were all there with me, that night.

■

EPILOGUE

« 17 »

Here in my jail cell, in the Walsenburg Jail, my door swings open.

Startled, I rise. Tomorrow is the day of my trial, not today.

"You're free to go, Ma'am," the warden tells me.

I stare at him; how can this be?

"Governor's orders." He leaves with a hint of a smile.

As I pack up my things, I think of Pratt, West Virginia.

Again, a governor has been forced to give way.

Tears of relief fill my eyes as I walk out into the sunlight. My jailors salute me as I pass. The light hurts my eyes; I shield them with my hand and head for the news stand. The cost of a paper seems higher since I was locked up — maybe I'm wrong. The date on the paper is April 17th, 1914.

And then I see the black smear of headlines: Here, in Colorado, as it was for so long in West Virginia, the coal mining wars smoulder on. I stand in a strike zone under martial law. For a moment, my shoulders sag; my limbs feel heavy. We slay one monster and another rises up somewhere else. Well, that's really not news, I tell myself. What did I expect? A brass band? Another night at Carnegie Hall?

As soon as I can, I must catch a train to Washington, D.C., where I will testify before Congress again. This time, I'll be sure to meet with the Rockefeller boy, John. The Colorado Fuel & Iron Company, owned by his family, runs many of that state's coal mines....

But soon, all such thoughts stop.

There are only three words left to speak:

The Ludlow Massacre.

Near that small Colorado town, 2,000 miners had formed a tent colony. There were two hundred tents, more than two hundred families. Three days after my release, the state militia set it on fire. It began with two bomb blasts. It ended in death. The militia had turned into a mob. All that terrible day, there was only gunfire and flames. Hiding in trenches, mothers with children burned alive. Then, in revenge, the strikers burned company property. President Wilson had sent in federal troops....

Those were the facts. In horror, I read them on a train. I could not eat, could not sleep. I tried to absorb the words in the papers; I tried to believe what I'd promised that night at Carnegie Hall:

"We shall go on."

~~

Somehow, we do.

Somehow, we are.

I am back in Colorado and here I remain, writing on my knee, traveling all over this troubled state. Everywhere I go, I tell the story of the Ludlow Massacre, and every day, I watch the nation's own horror build. I work constantly, raising money and garnering food for the strikers. So much undone — so much yet to do.

From the wreckage, once more, we try to rebuild. I should be used to this pattern by now. This has formed the shape of my life: Destruction and deliverance, locked in one dance. I would not call this a waltz through the parlor. But I would not want that, I know that, too.

There are so many different demands on my time, I am reminded of my days as a young wife and mother. I can think of those days with gratitude now, as well as pain. I've noticed this change since my stay in the Walsenburg jail. Near that jail, in the strike zone, new talks proceed. There is some reason for hope, after all. The people's spirits are not broken yet. When I spoke at a rally in Denver, five thousand people screamed with joy. If a crowd can do that, it can go on to do more. I hope to see many new dramas unfold.

I am close to eighty and I'm not slowing down.

Soon, I will meet with President Wilson at the White House. I only wish that Jim Ashcroft could be there, with the other mill children, as well. In a way, they will be — and all the others.

A long line of traveling companions follow me now, back through the decades. At the head of that line stands George and our children. I sense their presence with me, at last.

At the start of this writing, in the Walsenburg jail, I thought about Twine. I thought how something like a rope's simple strength comes down to me. That twin-like strength bore me up as I gazed into the deep well of the past. Now, once more, I grasp that twine, that rope, and swing out over another deep well. As long as I can, I'll look to the future. And I'll be saying what I've said all my life:

Pray for the dead and fight like hell for the living.

— END —

ACKNOWLEDGMENTS

I am indebted to many sources for this novel. Among them, I gratefully acknowledge the outstanding work of:

Elliot J. Gorn in his biography, *Mother Jones: The Most Dangerous Woman in America*;

Dale Fetherling in her biography, *Mother Jones: The Miners' Angel*;

Edward M. Steel, editor of *The Court-Martial of Mother Jones*;

Judith Pinkerton Josephson, author of *Mother Jones: Fierce Fighter for Workers' Rights*;

Philip F. Foner's informative book, *Women and the American Labor Movement*, as well as his collection, *Mother Jones Speaks: Speeches and Writings of a Working-Class Writer*;

and Mary Harris Jones, herself, in *The Autobiography of Mother Jones*, edited by Charles H. Kerr.

Betsy Harvey Kraft in her book, *Mother Jones: One Woman's Fight for Labor*.

I also express my deep gratitude to my friends and family for their steadfast support.

—MH

AUTHOR'S NOTE

This novel is, by definition, a work of fiction. I did not set out to write a biography, nor did I intend to create a history of the American Labor Movement, which came into its own as did Mother Jones. Of course, this story includes highlights of her wide-ranging and peripatetic career, along with quotes drawn from her autobiography, speeches and letters. I have also tried to set Jones's life into historical context.

Above all, however, I wanted this novel to have a particular focus: the woman herself.

While Mother Jones's achievements are worthy of honor and admiration, I approached her life from a personal angle. I wanted to portray a woman who repeatedly surmounted overwhelming, even catastrophic events — then turned herself in life-affirming directions. How and why did she do this, again and again?

No one can know precisely, of course. Some biographers conjecture that Mother Jones was driven by anger at her own reversals, or a desire for respectability, or a sense that she had nothing left to lose. While I respect biographical conjectures, my interpretation of Jones's

motivations are quite different. I support this interpretation with a careful examination of her life and writings.

First, there is the powerful root influence of Jones's
background. She grew up poor and disenfranchised in
British-ruled Ireland. As Mary Harris, she would have
known the tension between the wealthy landlords and the
poor, oppressed Catholic tenant farmers. Such tenant
farmers were members of her mother's family, the Cotters
of Inchigeelagh, County Cork. Young Mary's relationship
with her extended family was a close one.

Mary Harris heard also heard stories of her rebellious
paternal grandfather; probably a member of the Whiteboys, a secret society. In her autobiography, she writes
that he was hanged by the authorities for anti-British
activities. This image of her rebel grandfather, hanging
from a rope, made a strong impression on Mary Harris.
Her father, Richard Harris, is also recalled as a rebel who
fled British authorities to escape Ireland.

It is difficult to document the activities of poor,
illiterate people. It is even harder to document Irish
Catholic secret societies. In this area, I rely on Mother
Jones's autobiography, which has the ring of truth, for
me. Liberty from oppression was clearly a part of Mary
Harris Jones's early ethos. It seems quite natural that
she would later fight workers' exploitation by American
industrialists; here we may see parallels with the tension
between Irish landlords and their tenants farmers.

In addition, it is impossible to underestimate the
Great Famine's indelible impact on the young Mary
Harris Jones. This devastating historical event, of seismic
proportions, influenced the Harris family quite directly.
Mary would have seen the green-mouthed, grass-eating
poor who had died on the roads. Her family also struggled
to survive *The Great Hunger* itself. I believe that these

formative experiences influenced Jones's later vocational orientation, as well as her will to survive tragedy.

Second, and just as important, is the influence of George Jones, who married Mary Harris early in 1861 (some biographers report the date of 1860). He was an active and avid member of the International Iron Molders Union, founded by the admired William Sylvis. Jones knew the Sylvis credos and would have shared these with his wife.

Some sources indicate that George Jones was instrumental in the establishment of Local 66, the Memphis chapter of his union. In its note of his death, his union "brothers" refer to his energetic activities on their behalf. Mary Harris Jones was dedicated to her marriage, her husband and his ideas, which would have resonated strongly with those of her forebears. Later, she expressed her opinion that a wife should support her husband in his work, "so that he may remain resolute." As part of her support, she would have read her husband's union journal, delivered regularly to the Jones household.

After her husband's untimely death in October, 1867, Mary Harris Jones recalls how she "sat alone through nights of grief." It was her husband's union that came to her at this critical time. She never could have forgotten the intervention of Local 66. It was this union chapter that gave her husband a proper burial. Without Local 66, Jones's body would have been piled on the city's "death-carts," and buried in an anonymous mass grave.

George Jones's union also honored their "brother" by draping its local charter in black for thirty days, a moving gesture that would not have been lost on Mary Harris Jones. She herself wore a widow's black garb for the rest of her own long life. She never forgot her husband, though it was painful for her to speak of him. However, decades after his death, she spoke passionately about fighting the carrier of the disease that had killed her husband: Yellow Fever. The conjunction of a happy marriage with union ideals must have left a powerful legacy with George Jones's widow.

Third, it is also impossible to underestimate the impact of Mary Jones's four children on her life. Her involvement with them must have been intense, since they were born close together — and all four were under the age of six when they died, one by one, in the same week, just prior to their father's death.

In her autobiography, Mary Harris Jones writes poignantly about watching these children die and washing "their little bodies." On the eve of her death, so many year later, she said that she wished to live longer in order to stop "the sobbing of little children."

Mary Jones's personal maternal experience seems a clear root-cause for her passionate and persistent fight against child labor. "I love children," she often said. She also addressed her younger friend, Terence Powderly, as "my dear son." Of course, Powderly bore the same name as Jones's only son. It seems natural that she treasured — and perhaps helped to foster — her "professional," public title of "Mother."

Fourth, Mary Jones must have been strongly influenced by the devastation — personal and general — of the great Chicago fire of 1871. As a ruined, destitute, homeless widow, she must have felt an even greater kinship with the downtrodden; especially after huddling with the dispossessed in Old Saint Mary's Church for an extended interval.

This period has clear resonance with her memories of the Great Famine, years before. Once again, the poor and hungry wandered in the streets — but now, she was among them.

Three times, Mary Jones experienced the end of a personal world. After losing her family, her business, her homes in Memphis and Chicago, it seems inevitable that she would have considered giving up, even if this feeling passed briefly. In the wake of the fire, it seems highly significant to me that Jones did not turn to the Church or to her estranged siblings in Toronto.

Instead, Mary Jones turned to the labor movement — so closely associated with her husband and her forebears. Perhaps she felt she was bearing their cause into the future — as, in fact, she was. Perhaps, she carried on for the sakes of those she had lost. I believe historical evidence supports this interpretation: Mother Jones's work became a labor of fierce love, rather than personal rage at her own fate.

Her anger was directed at injustice and its perpetrators, a stance buttressed by the views of her forebears and her husband. Affection and tenderness is often expressed in her writings. Jones wrote about the miners as "her boys" — another indication of her maternal feelings toward those she aided. In my first novel, *A Woman Called Moses*, I noticed how Harriet Tubman's calling expanded beyond her immediate relatives to encompass a broader definition of family. Perhaps this same sense of expansion happened for Mother Mary Jones.

Mary Jones did more than survive — though that in itself is no small feat. She does not give evidence of bitterness or depression, which would have been understandable reactions to three catastrophic life-events. Instead, she managed to use her experiences to help others, over and over again. In her words and actions, she expressed her solidarity with the struggles of working people.

Even before she was hired by the United Mine Workers of America, she was fighting for the rights of laborers. It is notable that she also worked with and for African American miners; Italian, Mexican and Slavic immigrants; women, from miners' wives to silk-weavers, dressmakers to bottle washers; and consistently, for children.

After the violence in Ludlow, Colorado, she comforted widows as well as children. From what she wrote — and from what she omitted — I believe that Mother Jones always carried within her the pain of the past. It is difficult to imagine that anyone could blot out the devastating and traumatic events she experienced. Her response to them, however, is an inspiration to me and to many others.

Mother Jones continued her active work until 1924, when she turned eighty-seven. In that year, she participated in a Chicago dressmakers' strike — some fifty years after she herself had been a dressmaker in the city. In 1925, she wrote an account of her career in *The Autobiography of Mother Jones*. Her letters and speeches have also been collected and published (see acknowledgments). Until her death in 1930, she continued to speak out on labor-related issues.

The birth date of Mary Harris is somewhat problematic. She claimed this as May 1, 1830, although August 1, 1837 is the date on her baptismal records at Saint Mary's Roman Catholic Cathedral in Cork City, County Cork, Ireland. It is probable that Mother Jones adopted a May Day birth date for symbolic reasons, and added a few years to her age to augment her grandmotherly image, as some biographers suggest. This discrepancy in birth dates, however, causes further biographical discrepancies in dates of her life's events, including the exact year she emigrated to North America with her mother and siblings. (Her father had emigrated ahead of them, as was often the custom).

In most cases, I have followed the timeline set forth by Professor Elliot Gorn, in his biography of Mother Jones (see acknowledgments). In several sections, I have relied on the speeches, letters, and recollections of events by Mother Jones herself.

It is a fact that Mary Harris grew up in the slums of North Cork and spent time with her mother's family, the Cotters of Inchigeelah, thirty miles from Cork City. I have followed Mother Jones's account of her ancestors' rebel activities.

Early in 1861, Mary Harris married George Jones, a master iron molder and dedicated union member. No source disputes October, 1867, as the time of her husband's death, following those of their four small children, in the space of one week. This family perished in the Yellow Fever epidemic that swept Memphis, Tennessee and decimated the Jones's neighborhood, nicknamed "Pinch-gut." For the rest of her life, Mary Harris Jones wore black.
Unable to remain in Memphis, she moved to Chicago, although the date of that move is debatable. It is factual, however, that Chicago's Great Fire in October, 1871, destroyed Mary Jones's dressmaking shop and all that she owned. She became a homeless, childless, destitute widow at that time.

Mary Jones did take refuge in Old Saint Mary's Church, near the site of her burned-out Chicago home. Because of her strong family ties (on her maternal side) to the Cotters, long established in Inchigeelagh, County

Cork, and because the O'LEARY predominated there, it is likely that Mary Harris Jones knew Patrick and Catherine O'Leary who had emigrated to Chicago. They were all members of a strong Irish-Catholic immigrant community in that city, although they may have belonged to different parishes.

Mrs. O'Leary's cow was accused of starting the Chicago fire and this inaccurate story became a legend. In fact, the journalist who propagated this story later admitted the story was a falsehood. It is not known if the O'LEARY met with Jones under the circumstances I imagined here, but it is entirely possible. This scene is designed to show the strength of the Cork immigrants in the face of great discrimination. It also attempts to clear Cate O'Leary of false accusations that caused her to die "heartbroken," more than twenty years later, according to one of her descendants.

In the 1870s, several sources suggest that Jones supported herself as a seamstress. She would not dignify other rumors, used as smears, with a response. According to her autobiography, she states that she was drawn to America's nascent labor movement during that decade. She cites her involvement with the Knights of Labor, a rising national union, different from preceding guilds. The Knights opened membership to all trades, to unskilled workers, immigrants, African-Americans, and women.

It is possible that she joined a local chapter that was not yet officially chartered. Through this union, Mary Harris Jones did meet Terence Powderly, the Knights' eventual leader. Their correspondence documents a life-long friendship.

Existing sources cite various dates for the emergence of the title, "Mother Jones," but the moniker stayed with its bearer for at least thirty years.

Another phrase persistently followed Jones: "The most dangerous woman in American," coined by a United States district attorney, Reese Blizzard, in West Virginia.

Mother Jones spent her last years in the Washington, D.C. home of her dear friends, Terence and Emma Powderly. There, Mother Jones was surrounded by a lively, extended family, until the death of Terence Powderly in 1924. Suffering from severe rheumatism, Jones came to need more care than Mrs. Powderly could provide. Walter and Lillie Mae Burgess took their ailing friend into their home in Hyattsville, Maryland. (It seems that Mary Harris Jones remained estranged from her siblings throughout her adult life.)

During Mother Jones's final few years, she was an invalid; during her last six months, she was unable to leave her room. In 1930, at summer's end, her death seemed immanent. She received the Last Rites of the Catholic Church and died on November 30, in the Burgess home. A funeral Mass followed.

The death of Mother Jones made headlines throughout the country. As a train carried her casket from Maryland to her Illinois burial site, crowds turned out to offer a final farewell. Her passing was mourned across America. At her express request, she was buried in the Union Miners Cemetery in Mount Olivet, Illinois. Striking miners, murdered in Virden, Illinois, in 1898, were buried here when their bodies were denied interment in consecrated ground elsewhere.

This cemetery was created for them by the UMWA and a monument to "Mother Mary Jones" stands at her grave.

■

Critical acclaim for other works by Marcy Heidish

Novels:

- *A Woman Called Moses*, Houghton Mifflin Co.
  - The acclaimed historical novel based on the amazing life of Harriet Tubman, legendary conductor on the Underground Railroad.
  - A Literary Guild Alternate Selection
  - A TV Movie, starring Cicely Tyson.

Praise for *A Woman Called Moses:*
- *Publishers Weekly*: [Harriet Tubman's] "story has been told before, but never as eloquently, almost poetically, as here ... achingly real ...a strong narrative of a totally committed woman, one who speaks directly to our own desperate need to feel committed — and our wish that somewhere in the world there were more people like Harriet Tubman."
- *The Washington Post Book World*: "Profoundly rewarding...a daring work of the imagination."
- *Chicago Sun Times*: "Marcy Heidish has, almost uncannily, crawled into the skin and very mind of Harriet Tubman.... The dialogue sings with poetic beauty."

- *The Secret Annie Oakley*, New American Library.
  - Historical novel based on the life of the legendary sharpshooter.

Praise for *The Secret Annie Oakley:*
- *Kirkus Reviews*: "An immensely touching and cohesive fictional biography of the legendary sharpshooter... builds from exemplary research to a fresh portrait of a talented woman in crisis...a class act —as Heidish reconstructs. with color and drama, the choreography of the shows, the tone of the period, and the textures of a haunting past."
- *The Arizona Daily Star*: "Marcy Heidish is an imaginative, amazing writer. She's a magician with words.... Each character has been brought to life with a mere pen stroke; flesh and blood beings that are more than fiction.... A masterpiece of creative writing."
- *The Kansas City Star:* "An unforgettable story."

- **Witnesses**, Houghton Mifflin Co.
  - Historical novel based on the life of lay minister Anne Hutchinson, religious freedom advocate.

<u>Praise for *Witnesses:*</u>
- **The New York Times Book Review:** "....nothing ordinary about her creation of this remarkable woman. The novel abounds in literary grace, employing the voices of the times as though heard this minute."
- **The New Yorker Magazine:** "A striking novel...a compelling portrait."
- **The Washington Post:** "Pure pleasure. Anne Hutchinson is real; thanks to *Witnesses,* she at last assumes her proper place...in American history."
—Jonathan Yardley, Pulitzer Prize-winning critic.

- **Deadline**, St. Martin's Press.
  - Contemporary psychological novel with a "mystery" as a narrative line.
  - Nominee for prestigious national "Edgar" Award; fine reviews.

<u>Praise for *Deadline*:</u>
- **Washington Post:** "*Deadline* is a tense, well-turned tale, filled with authentic police and newspaper people. Heidish's taut, punchy style moves the story at lightning speed."
- **Kirkus Reviews:** "The high-tension plot is enhanced by sharply etched pictures, by many vivid characters, and by a crisp, clean, first-person style. Heidish imbues her haunting story and her gutsy heroine with a rare sense of tenderness and poignancy. An impressive mystery by a gifted writer."
- **St. Martin's Press:** "This wire-tight novel probes relentlessly, driving deep into psychological darkness and violent death. As the riveting story reaches its stunning conclusion, we see a complex woman forced to meet the ultimate deadline."

■ *The Torching*, Simon & Schuster.

- Contemporary literary novel, hardcover and paperback.

- Literary Guild Alternate Selection; laudatory reviews.

<u>Praise for *The Torching*</u>:

• ***Washington Post Book World***: "Flex your fingers, gentle readers. You're going to be turning pages for the next few hours.... Because of Heidish's skill, we get the full force of her double-whammy...in part due to the grace with which she weaves the present-day and the historical, but also because of her inventiveness at the book's close, the daring way she gets both strands of plot to unite.... Marcy Heidish is a stylish and intelligent novelist to boot, more than up to the dizzying, tale-spinning task that she set for herself here."

• ***Kirkus Reviews:*** "Shuddery mystery-suspense with supernatural overtones."

• ***Library Journal:*** "Intricately constructed...A deliciously spine-tingling, multi-layered literary mystery..."

• ***Publishers Weekly***: "Subtle and gratifying psychological suspense.... Penetrating characterizations ... Heidish impeccably orchestrates the historical and contemporary, the supernatural and psychological."

• ***Simon & Schuster:*** With this spellbinding tale of mysticism, horror, and history, a gifted, award-winning writer ... here gives us a novel to rival the works of Anne Rice, Alfred Hitchcock, or Edgar Allan Poe — a vivid tale of an eighteenth-century midwife ... sentenced to burn as a witch in the tiny town of Maidstone, Maryland.... *The Torching* is an unforgettable novel about the power of words..."

- **Miracles**, New American Library.
  - Historical novel based on the life of Mother Elizabeth Seton, first American-born canonized saint.

Praise for *Miracles*:

• New American Library: *Miracles* is a novel charged with the vitality of a life that saw many changes, and with the power of a love that took many forms...as a lonely daughter of a wealthy, indifferent man; a searching young woman; a contented matron embracing a marriage that produced five beloved children; a widow searching for new meaning to life.

• **The New York Times Book Review**: This appealing book, told from the point of view of a skeptical modern priest, moves swiftly through tragedy to triumph.

• **Kirkus Reviews:** Working delicately with a balance of Church hagiography and psychological insight, Heidish provides another strong focus on the root dilemma of female saints and achievers.

Non-Fiction Books:

- **Defiant Daughters: Christian Women of Conscience**, Liguori Publications.

Praise for *Defiant Daughters*:

• **Liguori Publications**: Joan of Arc, Immaculée Ilibagiza, Corrie ten Book, and Sojourner Truth are among those women whom best-selling author Marcy Heidish calls "Defiant Daughters."

This informative, challenging, and entertaining book spotlights the lives of more than 20 spiritual trailblazers and their responses to crises of conscience. They represent different races, denominations, and nations, but all are feisty —often fiery— and always faithful to their callings.

What motivated these "defiant daughters," who gave their all for God? Heidish seeks out the decisive juncture where they took a stand for conscience, regardless of the consequences. This stunning and compelling book will bring you face-to-face with an unforgettable female gallery of "profiles in courage."

- **Soul and the City**, WaterBrook Press, Random House imprint.
                    Praise for *Soul and the City*:
• "I actually started reading Marcy Heidish's *Soul and the City* on a subway train, and I must say it had exactly the effect she writes about. It gave me peace in the middle of the hurry, the rush, the loud noise of the city." – Rick Hamlin, executive editor of *Guideposts* and author of *Finding God on the A Train.*

• "… a rich and nuanced touring companion to rival any Michelin or Eyewitness guide—usable in any city of the world. Keep it close and…you will meet beauty and holiness no matter where you pause to look." – Leigh McLeroy, author of *The Beautiful Ache* and *The Sacred Ordinary.*

- **Who Cares? Simple Ways YOU Can Reach Out**, Ave Maria Press.
          An ideal resource for anyone interested in engaged spirituality.
          This practical book is designed to bring out the caring person in each of us. Heidish offers simple, specific ways to practice the art of caring, especially within our immediate circle of concern.

                    Praise for *Who Cares?*:
• **Cultural Information Service:** "Contains savvy insights and wisdom about service... This is an ideal resource for anyone interested in engaged spirituality."

• **Fredericksburg Free Lance-Star**: "Covers just about every topic imaginable on ways that people can reach out to one another ... [written] in an easy-to-follow simple-style prose."

■ *A Candle At Midnight*, Ave Maria Press.

Praise for *A Candle At Midnight*:
• "...fills a void in the popular literature about depression. ...Heidish recognizes that making one's way through the agony and terror of depression is a spiritual pilgrimage as well. Heidish has constructed a meaningful collection of readings, rituals, and suggestions that have great practical utility. I recommend this book to anyone." – Martha M. Manning, Author of *Undercurrents: A Life Beneath the Surface*.

• "Heidish honors modern medicine and spiritual healing in this compelling work." – Alen J. Salerian, M.D., Medical Director of the Washington Psychiatric Center.

• "A masterpiece!" – Rev. Nancy Eggert, Director of the Shalem Center for Spiritual Direction.

Short Pieces:
• Articles and book reviews published in *Ms.* Magazine, *GEO* Magazine, *The Washington Post*, *The Washington Star*, and various in-flight periodicals.

• "*The Pilgrim Who Stayed*," *GEO* Magazine, about Chartres Cathedral, widely translated into many languages.

• "*The Grand Dame of the Harbor*," about the Statue of Liberty, a highly acclaimed cover story for *GEO* Magazine.

This article is included in a textbook anthology designed to teach writing to college students.